The Devil's Domain

Understanding Spiritual Darkness

Matthew Allen

DeWard
for your journey

Acknowledgments:

I am so blessed to have a wonderful support group of individuals around me who are always such an encouragement to me as I work on projects like this. The idea for this book came from the shepherds at the Kettering Church of Christ in Kettering, Ohio. This material has been designed to help Christians concentrate on walking in and reflecting the light of Jesus Christ. Until we understand the depth of darkness we once dwelt in, we will never realize the blessing of living inside God's marvelous light. Thus, the need for us to understand spiritual darkness.

I am especially indebted to **Jim Grushon,** who shared his thoughts with me each week in his office over a warm cup of coffee. His insight on darkness and what it means to be lost in sin were invaluable. Jim is a gifted spiritual leader whose help was immeasurable as I wrote the basic outlines for each chapter. Jim, I could not have finished this project without you. I am also thankful for **Rich Walker,** whose advice on how to write a few chapters, really made a difference in how this book will be received.

Along with Jim and Rich, I want to thank my wife, **Becky Allen,** who is always there for me to bounce ideas off of. She does the hard work of editing and patiently transforms my roughly written paragraphs into an easy-to-read flow. Thanks Becky!

I also have great appreciation for the members of my classes at Kettering Church of Christ, who always do a great job in contributing to each class session. Your comments and insight were a great help to me as I made course adjustments on the material.

Thanks also to **Jim Canada,** a good friend who has been such an encouragement to me over the last few years. He eagerly accepted my request to proof the material and offered his suggestions to make this book even better. I really appreciate you Jim.

And finally, I would be remiss if I didn't include **Daniel De-Garmo** and DeWard Publishers for making this book available to you. I have been impressed with their professionalism and quality of their product. It is an honor to be published by them.

Thanks for your purchase of this book, and may it help you in your journey to God's wonderful, eternal kingdom.

But you are a chosen race, a royal priesthood, a holy nation, a people for his own possession, that you may proclaim the excellencies of him who called you out of darkness into his marvelous light. Once you were not a people, but now you are God's people, once you had not received mercy, but now you have received mercy. 1 Peter 2.9-10.

Darkness from Beginning to End

Introduction

Estamos bien en el refugio los 33. These seven words made up the first message sent from 33 miners trapped in a Chilean gold and copper mine after a probe sent from rescuers 2000 feet above broke through the ceiling of the room where they took refuge. Seventeen days before, August 5, 2010, the mine collapsed — trapping the men inside as they were eating lunch. Over the next few hours they desperately searched through the tunnels and ventilation shafts, only to find each way out blocked by rubble. There would be no escape. Reality set in. Completely cut off from the light and freedom of the outside world, they were essentially buried alive in the dark recesses of the earth. Surviving on just two teaspoons of tuna and one biscuit every two days, they washed down their "meals" with a small sip of spoiled milk. As time went by, the workers were forced to spread out their rations, first eating once every 24 hours, then every 48 hours, and finally, every 72 hours. After the milk supply was exhausted, workers were forced to drink contaminated water from truck radiators and mining equipment. But, worse than that was the darkness. It affected everything. To get a few moments of brief relief, the miners would use their electric lights — from headlamps, jury-rigged light bulbs, trucks and tractors, as a "treat" and a "reward" to "boost morale." As the days went by, all hope began to diminish. Every hour they honked one of their vehicles' horns, on the faint hope that somebody would hear. One miner said, "The days went one into another. The first week was bad, but the second week, that was terrible."[1]

Most of us would have a hard time identifying with the sheer terror and fear of the unknown of spending 69 days in such a dark and dreadful place. After his rescue and hospital examination, the first place Mario Sepulvedia took his family to visit was the bright, sunny Chilean beach.[2]

For most humans, perhaps there is nothing more dreaded and fearful than darkness. Darkness is often associated with gloom, murkiness, and obscurity. Most of us avoid it at all costs. Darkness is disorienting. There is no sense of direction. Darkness robs things of their identity. When there is true darkness, one cannot see things for what they are. Where darkness reigns, there may be unseen dangers present—just out of reach. Darkness isolates. From this emerges our fear of the unknown, and so our fear of the darkness.

We have been created to thrive in the light. We build rooms with large windows to allow natural light to flow in. We love to bask in the warmth of the sun on a lazy summer day. We paint our rooms with bright and bold colors that enhance the artificial light inside. For seven months out of the year, we attempt to make the days feel longer with daylight savings time. Those who live in higher latitudes often flee to brighter, warmer confines during the short, cold days of winter. Prolonged exposure to darkness can drive people mad and make them depressed. When we are in the light, we tend to be happier, more content, and more productive. "Light is sweet, and it is pleasant for the eyes to see the sun." Ecclesiastes 11.7

Understanding Spiritual Darkness

God's word has much to say about darkness and light. *Light* is used as a symbol of God's purity, wisdom, and glory. Darkness is the exact opposite. In scripture, *darkness* is used to refer to the absence of God, the absence of knowledge, and the personal, active opposition to God's truth. In 2 Peter 1.19 *dark* is used to describe a "squalid, dirty place, that is destitute of brightness." It is also used to refer to a time of punishment, as in the *day of the Lord*. It can refer to things mysterious, trouble and affliction, death, or nothingness. Satan and his angels are said to be darkness—who live to increase their influence over all the earth. As a result, spiritual darkness is not passive. Rather, it is promoted by Satan and is diametrically opposed to Jesus' Lordship, the cross, God's word, and every Christian that walks on the face of the earth. In this sense, darkness is viewed as a threat—always encroaching on those who are in the light.

Light and darkness are described as polar opposites. Isaiah said: "The people who walked in darkness have seen a great light; those who dwelt in a land of deep darkness, on them has light shined." Isaiah 9.2.

There is no blending of the two. In the land of Israel this was literally true. "Day and night, light and darkness, are notable antitheses in Palestine. There the day does not slowly fade away into the night after a period of twilight, but before sunset there is the brightness of day, and when the sun has disappeared everything has changed and night is at hand. From sunset until the darkness of night is less than an hour."[3]

One either dwells in the light or the darkness. God's children have been called not to "walk in darkness," but must come out of "darkness" by placing their trust in the light and "walking in the light," as He is in the "light," (John 8.12; 12.35-36; 1 John 1.6-7). **Neutrality is impossible.** Either people remain in darkness and sin or, they place their trust in the light, and are rescued from the domain of darkness.

Darkness is the Absence of God

The simple definition of *darkness* is the "absence of light." Applying this definition to the spiritual, we may simply define *darkness* as the absence of God. "God is light, and in Him is no darkness at all." 1 John 1.5. In the Bible, we are first introduced to darkness in Genesis 1: In the beginning, God created the heavens and the earth. The earth was without form and void, and darkness was over the face of the deep. And the Spirit of God was hovering over the face of the waters. And God said, "Let there be light," and there was light. And God saw that the light was good. And God separated the light from the darkness. God called the light Day, and the darkness he called Night. And there was evening and there was morning, the first day." Genesis 1.1-5.

It is noteworthy that the Holy Spirit uses *darkness* to describe the condition present before creation. Before God hovered over the face of the waters, darkness prevailed. Not only does darkness represent the absence of God, but also the absence of every principle of nature mankind takes for granted. Simply stated, there was nothing. Darkness is a void. It is the absence of substance.

When God came, He brought order and principles. What had been void, now had substance. What was out of order now had purpose. What had been out of control and overpowering (darkness), was now under control. Where there had been no life, now, because of the absence of darkness, life was able to exist. Where there had been no law, now law exists. Relating to God's power, John said, "the light shines in the darkness, and the darkness has not overcome it." John 1.5. The presence of God dispels the darkness and brings peace, order, and life to all who are around it.

The worst part of the human existence is the feeling of loneliness. In scripture, darkness and loneliness are closely intertwined. The absence of God brings great despair and grief. Nothing could drive biblical characters to despondency quicker than the feeling that God had deserted them. Job asked God, "Why do you hide your face and count me as your enemy?" Job 13.24.

Before his afflictions, Job felt near to God. But afterward, it felt as if He had withdrawn from him which led him into deep spiritual darkness. "Oh, that I were as in the months of old, as in the days when God watched over me, when his lamp shone upon my head, and by his light I walked through darkness." Job 29.2-3. David also lamented the hiding of God's face. "How long, O LORD? Will you forget me forever? How long will you hide your face from me? How long must I take counsel in my soul and have sorrow in my heart all the day?" Psalm 13.1-2.

When God is gone, there is nothing left. The world is left only with darkness and there is no light. In his darkest hours, Jeremiah felt as if God had deserted him: "I am the man who has seen affliction under the rod of his wrath; he has driven and brought me into darkness without any light." Lamentations 3.1–2.

On the most monumental day in human history, Jesus was forced to experience the darkness that is associated with separation from God. As Jesus bore the penalty of our sin, God turned His face away. Darkness descended and in the silence of the moment, Jesus cried out, "My God, My God, why have You forsaken Me?" Matthew 27.46

Darkness is the Absence of Knowledge

In the Psalms, those without knowledge or understanding are said to "walk about in darkness," 82.5. Throughout God's Word, ignorance and falsehood are continually represented by *darkness.* Darkness effects what a person knows and believes. The absence of true knowledge is often referred to as *blindness.* Paul spoke of this when he said, "The god of this world has blinded the minds of the unbelievers, to keep them from seeing the light of the gospel of the glory of Christ, who is the image of God." 2 Corinthians 4.4. See also Romans 1.21 and Ephesians 4.18. Spiritual blindness is often revealed by how a person acts. Isaiah said, "Woe to those who call evil good and good evil, who put darkness for light and light for darkness." Isaiah 5.20.

Not only were the teachings of those in Judah corrupt, but their actions were as well. Spiritual blindness (dwelling in darkness) led to Paul's admonition in Romans 13.12-14.

In contrast, think of the imagery used in connection with God's way of truth.

Psalm 43.3: Send out your light and your truth; let them lead me; let them bring me to your holy hill and to your dwelling!

Psalm 119.105: Your word is a lamp to my feet and a light to my path.

Proverbs 4.18: the path of the righteous is like the light of dawn, which shines brighter and brighter until full day.

Proverbs 6.23: For the commandment is a lamp and the teaching a light, and the reproofs of discipline are the way of life.

Acts 26.17-18: I am sending you to open their eyes, so that they may turn from darkness to light and from the power of Satan to God, that they may receive forgiveness of sins and place among those who are sanctified by faith in me.

2 Corinthians 4.6: For God, who said, "Let light shine out of darkness," has shone in our hearts to give the light of the knowledge of the glory of God in the face of Jesus Christ.

1 John 2.11: Whoever hates his brother is in the darkness and walks in the darkness, and does not know where he is going, because the darkness has blinded his eyes.

We Are At War With the Forces of Darkness

Darkness is also used in scripture to describe those in open rebellion against God and His way. Satan and his servants are darkness and actively work to hinder God's purposes from being accomplished. Paul said we are at war "against the authorities, against the cosmic powers over this present darkness, against the spiritual forces of evil in the heavenly places." Ephesians 6.12. Satan is constantly on the offensive. In this sense, darkness is never passive. The threat is ever-present. It lurks. It crouches. It skulks and slinks behind. It waits for the optimum opportunity.

It is sobering, but it is important to remember we were once darkness. "At one time you were darkness, but now you are light in the Lord." Ephesians 5.8. Again, we are either "in" or "out" of darkness. There is no middle ground. Before we came to Christ, our entire existence was characterized by darkness. John MacArthur has written, "There was no other aspect to our spiritual life than that of darkness. We were children of darkness and sons of disobedience. We were not simply victims of Satan's system but were contributors to it. We were not merely in sin; our very nature was characterized by sin." [4] "Now, as God's sons and daughters, we are no longer in the darkness. For you are all children of light, children of the day. We are not of the night or of the darkness." 1 Thessalonians 5.5.

God's Punishment is Darkness

In the waning days of the northern kingdom, Amos pointed to a day of judgment and punishment. "Is not the day of the Lord darkness, and not light, and gloom with no brightness in it, Amos 5.20." Just over a century later, Ezekiel prophesied a day of doom for the people of Judah: "All the bright lights of heaven will I make dark over you and put darkness on your land, declares the Lord God." Ezekiel 32.8. These were terrible days where the judgment of God was poured out on the wicked. After repeated warnings of destruction and countless urgings to repent and return to God, the cities of Israel and Judah were destroyed and the people were carried off into captivity. "If one looks to the land, behold, darkness and distress; and the light is darkened by its clouds." Isaiah 5.30. These are just a few of hundreds of references in the Old Testament that warn of the completeness of Israel's destruction and their ultimate separation from God.

In the New Testament, *darkness* is used to describe eternal punishment. In some places, the term *outer darkness* is used. Where it is, this imagery is employed in the context of believers, the people of God. Those who profess belief but do not actually reflect God's purposes for His people are cast out into the outer darkness. Jesus used the term on three occasions to describe the ultimate destination of those who rebel against God. "In that place" of outer darkness, "there will be weeping and gnashing of teeth." Matthew 25.30b. Note the imagery of what awaits false teachers and those who sow discord in the church: "For if God did not spare angels when they sinned, but cast them into hell and committed them to chains of gloomy darkness to be kept until the judgment; and These are waterless springs and mists driven by a storm. For them the gloom of utter darkness has been reserved." 2 Peter 2.4, 17.

Jude also uses the same terminology in 1.6, 13. "For those who abide in darkness, the day of judgment and its result will be anything but pleasant."

We Must Avoid Spiritual Darkness at All Costs

After being *as good as dead,* the last place Chilean miner, Omar Reygaldas, wants to be is back in the oppressive darkness of a copper mine. He now travels throughout Chile and the world giving motivational speeches "to show the meaning of teamwork, power, and faith." The nightmares of his experience still haunt him. "I try to read, to tire myself out so that I can sleep well. But if I'm alone in a closed space it still makes me anxious—I have to get out and find someone to talk with or distract myself with something."[5] Rather than returning to the mine, other survivors are running their own small businesses selling fruits and vegetables, and others have spent time traveling and doing odd jobs as they deal with the emotional baggage associated with their traumatic experience.

With our response of faith in the saving power of Jesus, God has brought us into His marvelous light, 1 Peter 2.9. With every fiber of our being, we must resolve to fight off darkness at every turn. We are not alone in this war. We stand in the strength of Jesus and wear the protective armor of God. With God on our side, we are guaranteed victory over darkness. The only way the darkness will overtake us is if we surrender to it. Heighten your commitment to Christ. Hold on to God's hand each day. Trust in God no matter what. Satan will give it his best shot, but you don't have to become his prey.

For Thought and Reflection:

- What scares you most about darkness?

- How does darkness affect our emotions?

- Define *darkness* and *light* as used in scripture.

- Can one be in *darkness* and *light* at the same time?

- Describe the characteristics of darkness before creation.

- How did light change our physical world? Are there any spiritual applications?

- How are men and women affected by the absence of God?

- Describe the activity of darkness. Is it passive or aggressive?

- What is *outer darkness* as described by Jesus?

- How can *darkness* overtake us?

Light Dispels Darkness

Introduction

In today's modern world, perhaps there is no greater example of a failed state than Somalia. Located on the horn of Africa, Somalia has a rich cultural and ancestral history dating back to the 9th century. Before colonization by Europeans, its capitol, Mogadishu, was a flourishing trading port on Africa's Indian Ocean coast. During the 18th century, the city fell into decline and has never recovered. Achieving independence from Great Britain in 1960, Somalia has been constantly plagued by clan rivalries, corruption, dictators, and manipulation by foreign powers. The nation has remained underdeveloped and very poor, and a decade into the 21st century, things have only gotten worse. In 1991 the government of Said Barre failed, launching Somalia into a brutal civil war between two warlords. Compounding the problem was the worst African drought in over a century, which created a devastating famine that took over 300,000 lives in 1992 alone. Since then, there has been no national government powerful enough to deal with the lawless factions inside the country. Thugs and warlords rule everywhere. Chaos reigns. Life is cheap. For most, death finds its prey easy and often. Nearly all of the cultured and educated class are dead or have fled. One in five Somalis is a refugee, most of them living within the borders of their own country. There are plagues among the people and cattle. Starvation is widespread. Mogadishu has been reduced to rubble. Today, there are no government buildings, no public hospitals, camels graze on the only runway at the international airport, and vehicles are constantly stopped at roadblocks every few kilometers where armed thugs use AK-47's to extort money.[6]

Somalia is a tragic, real-life example of how lawlessness and the ignoring of God's basic principles lead to chaos. For most of us, this part of Africa will never make it onto our wish list of exotic places to travel—and with good reason. Darkness has descended over this tiny country and it has become completely isolated from the rest of the world. If there ever were an example of the hopelessness that darkness represents, Somalia would be it.

Previously, we learned how darkness is associated with gloominess, dread, and fear. Most of us avoid darkness at all costs. Making the application to *spiritual darkness,* we can observe how God's word uses this term to explain the absence of God and knowledge, Satan and those who rebel against God's truth, and the judgment of God. We have learned how light and darkness are polar opposites. There is no blending of the two. One either dwells in the light or the darkness. Neutrality is impossible. "If we say we have fellowship with him while we walk in darkness, we lie and do not practice the truth. But if we walk in the light, as he is in the light, we have fellowship with one another, and the blood of Jesus his Son cleanses us from all sin." 1 John 1.6-7.

We have also looked at Genesis 1.1-5. Here, *darkness* is used to describe the conditions present before creation. Simply stated, before creation there was *nothing.* While this may sound blatantly obvious, it is very important to understand when we examine the characteristics of darkness. Darkness is a *void.* It represents chaos and the absence of substance.

Light represents God and all that is good. *Light* represents purity, wisdom, and righteousness. Using the creation account as our reference, we see the power of light—literally and spiritually. When God came, lawlessness was replaced with order and the establishment of principles. Substance replaced void. Purpose replaced chaos. What was unsettled and dead was now replaced with peace and life.

Order. Substance. Purpose. Peace. Life. All of these spiritual qualities were in abundance as Adam and Eve got used to the confines of living inside the Garden of Eden. They were in close fellowship and union with God. The presence of God was with them in the garden, Genesis 3.8. All of creation was perfect and lived in harmony. Life was good in the warmth of God's light. Then, faster than a bolt of lightning, everything changed. Adam and Eve chose to succumb to temptation. Sin separated them from God and spiritual darkness reigned. Ever since that fateful moment in the garden, our world has been subjected to darkness, desolation and destruction. Isaiah said, "the way of peace they do not know, and there is no justice in their paths; they have made their roads crooked; no one who treads on them knows peace. ... We hope for light, and behold, darkness, and for brightness, but we walk in gloom. We grope for the wall like the blind; we grope like those who have no eyes; we stumble at noon as in the twilight, among those in full vigor we are like dead men." Isaiah 59.9-10.

After the fall of man, God enacted His bold plan to redeem us from sin. Through Jesus, God forever dispelled spiritual darkness and things have never been the same. In this lesson, we will examine how God brought light to Israel, and ultimately to everyone through the gift of His Son, Jesus.

How God Brought Light to Ancient Israel

When God delivered the Hebrews from Egypt, He brought light to their world. We need to realize what God had to work with. In many ways, the Hebrews were out of control, undisciplined, disorganized, and distrustful. During their 400 years of captivity, the Hebrews adopted many facets of Egyptian culture as their own—including the darkness of Egypt's religious calf-worshipping cults.

The fact of Israelites worship and homage toward Egyptian gods is well documented. Upon entering Canaan, Joshua told the Israelites to "put away the gods that your fathers served beyond the River and in Egypt, and serve the Lord." Joshua 24.14b. But, from the very beginning of their liberation, this was a problem. In Exodus 32, when Moses was delayed on the mountain longer than the people expected, is it a mere coincidence that Aaron created an idol in the shape of a golden calf? His actions suggest he was falling back on what he had been familiar with in Egypt. The

Egyptians worshipped living bulls as incarnations of Ptah and Ra. Elaborate rituals were connected with the life-size image of the Hathor-cow. The sun was revered as the "valiant bull" and the reigning Pharaoh as the "Bull of Bulls." Many of the Hebrews would have been familiar with the rites of Mnevis' feast at Heliopolis, which included boisterous revelry, dancing, offerings, etc. After Aaron presented the golden calf to the people, the people reveled and celebrated—probably in the same ways they were familiar with in Egypt, Exodus 32.4-6. In the New Testament, Stephen recounted their idolatry.[7] "Make for us gods who will go before us. As for this Moses who led us out from the land of Egypt, we do not know what has become of him. And they made a calf in those days, and offered a sacrifice to the idol and were rejoicing in the works of their hands." Acts 7.40-41.

Because they had been living in spiritual darkness, Israel had to learn the basics of right and wrong. The moral law is summarized in the ten commandments. The first command is significant. *You shall have no other gods before me.* If Israel was going to come out of the darkness, they would have to set God at the forefront of their lives, as God intended to redefine their concept of who and what to worship. The second command further clarifies His expectations: "You shall not make for yourself a carved image, or any likeness of anything that is in heaven above, or that is in the earth beneath, or that is in the water under the earth." Exodus 20.3-4.

In bringing light, God gave an out of control people a legal system. The law specifically pertained to their situation and needs. It regulated their lives completely. It was all for their good. "If you obey the commandments of the LORD your God that I command you today, by loving the LORD your God, by walking in his ways, and by keeping his commandments and his statutes and his rules, then you shall live and multiply, and the LORD your God will bless you in the land that you are entering to take possession of it." Deuteronomy 30.16. The law promoted justice, physical health, honesty, and compassion. Because they had entered God's light, Israel stood far above the darkness of godless nations around them.

The light God provided also gave a people who had no purpose a mission. Through the lineage of Abraham, Isaac, Jacob, and hundreds of other Hebrews, Israel would bring forth God's greatest gift and source of eternal light: Jesus, John 1.1-5.

How God Brought Eternal Light to Our World

Four hundred years before the coming of Christ, God's people were drowning in discouragement and disillusionment. The forces of spiritual darkness seemed to prevail. Those who were stubbornly arrogant and refused to submit to God seemed to have the advantage. "Evildoers not only prosper but they put God to the test and they escape." Malachi 3.15. God reassured the faithful that there was (and is) a day coming when those evildoers would be punished. They would be destroyed: "the day is coming, burning like an oven, when all the arrogant and all evildoers will be stubble. The day that is coming...will leave them neither root nor branch." Malachi 4.1.

God's message in Malachi builds to a crescendo with a significant Messianic prophecy. The imagery of the Holy Spirit's language is striking. In 4.2a, Jesus is referred to as the "sun of righteousness" who will "rise with healing in his wings." The eternal light of Jesus would dispel the spiritual darkness. The power of Jesus' light would turn gloom into joy: "You shall go out leaping like calves from the stall." 4.2b. The power of Jesus' light would render the wicked insignificant, "You shall tread down the wicked, for they will be ashes under the soles of your feet." 4.3a. No longer would evil reign unchecked. No longer would Satan dominate.

Could this prophecy in Malachi be what inspired Zechariah's foretelling of the mission of John the Baptist? "And you, child, will be called the prophet of the Most High; for you will go before the Lord to prepare His ways, to give knowledge of salvation to His people in the forgiveness of their sins, because of the tender mercy of our God, whereby the sunrise shall visit us from on high." Luke 1.76-78. Jesus is the light that dispels the darkness; the warmth that takes away the cold, and the joy that casts out gloom. He is the calm that takes away the storm and the judge who punishes the unrighteous. Isaiah said, "The people who walked in darkness have seen a great light; those who dwelt in a land of deep darkness on them has light shone." Isaiah 9.2. It was this passage that Matthew referred to as Jesus began His public ministry, Matthew 4.14-16. John also identified Jesus' credentials as light in John 1.4-5.

As Jesus' ministry progressed, He was very candid in referring to Himself as Light. "I am the light of the world. Whoever follows Me will not walk in darkness, but will have the light of life." John 8.12. He was the one about which the prophets had long looked forward to.[8] *He* was the one who would fulfill the Father's purposes in restoring mankind's lost relationship with God.[9] *He* was the one who would crush Satan and the forces of darkness by giving eternal life to those who live by faith.[10] He was "the lamb of God that would take away the sins of the world." John 1.29.

The significance of John 8.12 must not be missed. Jesus is **the** light, not simply "a" light or "another" light. Jesus does not say that He is holding the light, or that He has the light, or that He is the way to the light. He declares that He is the **one** and **only** light of the world.[11]

Spiritual Darkness Cannot Overcome Jesus' Light

While on earth, Satan took his best shot at derailing Jesus' mission. The ordeal Jesus endured in Matthew 4.1-11 was not the only time Satan tempted Jesus. As the cross drew nearer, Satan stepped up his attacks, even using Jesus' closest and most dedicated disciples against Him, Matthew 16.23. Can you imagine the level of temptation Satan administered on the night before Jesus' death? During the scourging? On the way to Golgatha? Equipping us for our own spiritual battles, the Bible clearly shows us the key to Jesus' success: total focus on His mission and the subjugation of His personal desires to His Father's, John 5.19-20, 30; 6.38; 12.27; 17.1-4. **Nothing** was going to deter Jesus from His mission. *Light* is more powerful than *darkness*.

In our physical world, nothing is more powerful than death. Everyone dies. It is fitting that *darkness* is so closely associated with death. To us, death is mysterious and obscure. From our vantage point, we cannot see past it. The unknowns associated with death generate fear. From a physical perspective, victory over death is hopeless. No one has overcome it. No one, except Jesus. Paul uses *death* to describe our spiritual condition while Satan controlled our heart. "We were dead in our trespasses and sin." Ephesians 2.1. Our situation was hopeless. In and of ourselves there was no way out. But, through Jesus, God brought eternal life to a world that had been spiritually dead since that dreadful day in the garden of Eden. "In Him was life, and the life was the light of men." John 1.4. The light of Jesus dispelled our darkness and we have been made "alive together with Christ." Ephesians 2.5. What was *impossible* is *possible* through Jesus. Light is more powerful than darkness.

Now, through the power of Christ and our willing hearts, we will be transformed into the image of Christ, Colossians 3.5-17, Romans 8.29. We manifest the effects of light in our individual lives, our families, on the job, and inside our community. God's incredible light dispels the darkness and changes the world one life at a time. Through His glorious gospel, Jesus brings order, peace, and harmony to a dark world.

It is important to remember that our coming into the light will be met with severe resistance. As light ascends on the horizon, it reveals what darkness has concealed. Although Satan was defeated by the work of Jesus on the cross and His resurrection, Satan and his demonic forces live to make war against Christians. While destruction in the fire of hell is their ultimate destiny, they have made it their goal to take as many with them as they can. "Your adversary the devil prowls around like a roaring lion, seeking someone to devour." 1 Peter 5.8. We must never forget that though the forces of darkness may resist, they can **never** overcome. *Light* is more powerful than *darkness*.

While darkness is powerful and is not passive, its abilities are limited. In John's gospel, we learn an important fact. "The light shines in the darkness, and the darkness has not overcome it." John 1.5. The key word in this verse is *overcome*. In the original language *overcome* is a compound word. The first part of the word carries the force of something that is "dominating," or "subjugating." The second part of the word means to "seize," or "grab hold of." When these two words are placed together, the meaning is "to pull down, seize, tackle, conquer, or to hold under one's power." By using this word, John teaches us that *darkness does not have the ability to suppress or hold the light under its domain.*[12]

As long as we *walk in the light* we can live with confidence and assurance of our salvation, 1 John 1.7-10, 2.1-5. When we resist by drawing near to God, Satan and the forces of darkness will flee. "Submit yourselves therefore to God. Resist the devil, and he will flee from you. Draw near to God, and He will draw near to you." James 4.7-8a. When we put on God's armor of protection, we will be "able to stand against the schemes of the devil." Ephesians 6.11.

Conclusion

In modern-day Somalia, *darkness* reigns. Lawlessness has isolated the country from the rest of the world. Evil and death prevail. Hopelessness abounds in this, the *darkest* corner of Africa.

Likewise, the forces of spiritual darkness rob us of our sense of order, purpose, peace, and life. These things lead to hopelessness and despair, resulting in destruction and eternal death. But, Satan and his surrogates are no match for the powerful light of Christ. Jesus has dispelled the darkness and rendered the devil's lasting power impotent.

We can learn much about *darkness* by examining how it is dispelled by light. Open your heart to God. Raise the level of your commitment and heighten your desire to always dwell in God's all powerful and eternal light.

For Thought and Reflection:

- Briefly describe and contrast *darkness* and *light*.

- What spiritual qualities were abundantly present in the garden before the fall of man?

- When God led them out of Egypt, in what ways were the Hebrew people out of control, disorganized, undisciplined, and distrustful?

- How did the law completely regulate the lives of the Israelites?

- What was the purpose of the law?

- Who is the *sun of righteousness?* Explain why Malachi's prophecy is so significant.

- Why is John 8.12 such a vital passage in God's word?

- Why is death a fitting description of our spiritual condition before we were remade through Jesus?

- Describe the meaning of *overcome* as used in John 1.5. How does this help you in your understanding of *darkness?*

- How can we live with confidence and assurance as we walk in the light?

How Darkness Attracts Us

Introduction

On January 3, 2011, a reporter with the *Columbus Dispatch* recorded an interview with Ted Williams, a down-on-his-luck radio commentator who had become homeless after losing his job due to drug and alcohol abuse. The interview was posted on YouTube and quickly went viral. Just three days later, January 6, 2011, the country was riveted with Ted's story and his "golden voice." Williams was quickly offered employment with the Cleveland Cavaliers basketball franchise and flown to New York, appearing on NBC's Today show doing the voice-over intro as the show came on the air. His quick rise to fame was incredible. Imagine being homeless, living on the cold and snowy streets of Columbus, and ending the week inside a posh New York hotel — conducting media interviews and doing advertising spots for nationally known companies. Hollywood called and by the weekend Williams found himself out on the west coast. By January 12, in an interview with *Dr. Phil*, Williams admitted to drinking heavily during his rocket ride to fame and voluntarily checked into rehab. Twelve days later he checked himself out and by the middle of the year, found himself back in a rehab again — after falling prey to narcotics abuse.

Williams' story is one of great tragedy but also one of great hope. His substance abuse cost him *everything*. He lost his marriage, his relationship with his children and with his mother. He wasted an unbelievable amount of money and lost his career numerous times. Blessed with tremendous opportunities, why does Williams keep throwing it away? How does he seem to lose battle after battle? What is so attractive about the darkness that he makes the decision to run back into it, time after time? His struggle — is the same one we face — with different *issues* and without national media attention and 24/7 internet exposure.

What is our attraction with darkness? Especially, after coming out of it into God's marvelous light. Imagine being lost inside an abandoned mine. As you desperately try to find your way out, wandering around in the darkness you actually go down deeper. Every tunnel leads to a dead end, or to another tunnel. Frustration sets in as you have no idea of which way to go. Your eyes are wide open, but all you see is black darkness. You are cold, damp, and dirty. There is no place to rest. Then, after a week you catch a faint glimpse of light and with every ounce of remaining energy, you make your way to the light and find yourself outside. The light is bright, so bright in fact that it hurts your eyes. You begin to wonder, *am I really better off?* Your mind wanders back to a few things inside the mine that gave temporary enjoyment by distracting you from where you were. So, you make the decision to go back down into the mine and live. This story, though hard to believe, is repeated countless times everyday — in a much more serious way. As people see the light of the gospel and spiritual life, and then go back to the old way of darkness and death. [13]

Previously, we have attempted to define spiritual darkness. We have seen how it represents the absence of God and His truth. It also stands for the activity of Satan and those in the demonic realm who make war with everything that is pure, just, and holy. In our world, the battleground is inside the hearts and minds of men and women. Spiritual darkness is not passive. It creeps, skulks, and slinks behind looking for a way to exploit the passions of our flesh, moving us to carry out the desires of the body and mind, Ephesians 2.3. While darkness creeps, we also have a tendency to gravitate toward it as well.

We are caught inside a vice, wedged between two great forces that intend to squeeze us into submission and make us their master. As Satan advances on one side, on the other side we contend with our human will and the flesh. While it may feel as if victory is impossible, God promises to equip us with all the tools we need to engage the enemy in every spiritual battle we face. And as we wield every punch, deity stands with us, fighting along side us—guaranteeing us victory. "I will never leave you or forsake you." Hebrews 13.5. Defeat is only an option when we choose to stand down and allow Satan to have his way. Unfortunately, most of the time, all Satan has to do is walk right in the door we've left unlocked and wide open, due to the desire of our eyes and flesh, and the pride of life. 1 John 2.16.

What causes us to leave the door open where Satan comes in, at worst without any opposition, or at best, with weak resistance? Why do we find ourselves so easily squeezed and crushed by Satan and his forces of darkness? In this lesson we will take a look at three ways darkness attracts.

Satan Cloaks Bondage Inside the Promise of Freedom

After a decade or more of marriage, what makes a husband or wife wake up one morning and decide that it's time to go? What moves them to determine that they *just don't love their spouse anymore* and that *they no longer want to be married?* What could cause them to betray the one they once promised to love and cherish *forever* and willfully step outside of the marriage to find fulfillment? What could cause a father or mother to brazenly crush their children into a million emotional pieces as they break up a marriage? As the fighting intensifies, the children cry, and the family crumbles, and Satan smiles. This awful scene replays itself every day in today's society. And while we are not often surprised to see it happen inside families void of a relationship with Christ, it also happens with regular occurrence inside Christian households. Never say never. It *could* happen to you, *if* you allow Satan to wrap up his shackles and chains inside a custom wrapped, shiny package of "freedom."

From the very beginning, Satan has used his cunning and deceptive practices to make God's way appear restrictive, antiquated, prude, and binding. Think of how he got to Eve that day inside the garden. Eve clearly knew God's expectations regarding the eating of the fruit from the tree of life. She did not wake up that morning expecting to disobey God. But, Satan knew exactly how to set his trap. *He promised freedom.* He deceived her into thinking the blessings of her present situation were undesirable and that there was something far better on the other side. Notice how Satan worked: "You will not surely die. For God knows that when you eat of it your eyes will be opened, and you will be like God, knowing good and evil." Genesis 3.4-5. We can easily see how he made it sound as if God was hiding something that she deserved and that life would be so much better once she took what was *rightfully* hers. Once he convinced her that she would be more fulfilled and experience unbridled freedom apart from the constriction of God's rules, it was all but over. She was clearly in his trap. But, she had yet to follow through. What pushed her over the edge? What made her pull the fruit off the tree and eat?

"So when the woman saw that the tree was good for food, and that it was a delight to the eyes, and that the tree was to be desired to make one wise, she took of its fruit and ate, and she also gave some to her husband who was with her, and he ate." Genesis 3.6. You can almost see the vice closing in on Eve. Already convinced that she deserved freedom, now the problem of the fleshly desire kicked in. She quickly rationalized that the fruit could be eaten, and that it looked *really* good. The physical desire of the flesh, coupled with a powerful lie, proved to be a lethal combination. She and her husband were crushed by Satan. Instead of a life of peace, freedom and bliss, they were separated from God and spent the rest of their days moving closer to their death, Genesis 3.16-24. Never underestimate the power of the flesh and the power of our own self will when coupled with Satan's lies.

The great tragedy is that only after sin has occured and one is trapped, that true bondage and confinement begins. What looked so great on the front end could not have turned out worse. Satan's tactics have never changed. The process that worked so effectively with Eve plays out day after day in the lives of countless people.

Those in Darkness Applaud Evil

In writing about the former life of Christians Paul says, "we all once lived in the passions of our flesh, carrying out the desires of the body and the mind, and were by nature children of wrath, like the rest of mankind." Ephesians 2.3. It is hard to think about, but in essence we were once pawns of Satan. His intent was to use us to further his purposes by making the lives of those around us more evil.

Now that we are in Christ, Satan tempts us to come back under the shroud of his darkness through the hearty approval of those who are already trapped by him. Those in the demonic world and those controlled by the dark power on earth cheer us on as we take backward steps—away from God and His light. Satan is not neutral. His ways are *always* negative. He constantly looks for a way to use darkness to make our spiritual lives unstable. In fact, we need to understand that darkness is *militant*. It never ceases to provide or encourage opportunities for more sin and depravity.

"Let no one deceive you with empty words, for because of these things the wrath of God comes upon the sons of disobedience. Therefore do not become partners with them; for at one time you were darkness, but now you are light in the Lord. Walk as children of light (for the fruit of light is found in all that is good and right and true), and try to discern what is pleasing to the Lord." Ephesians 5.6–10. What Paul says in verse 6 is especially important. *Let no one deceive you with empty words.* Those already in darkness work to convince us that sin is not ugly, or dirty and repulsive. Think of how every effort is made to avoid the word *sin* altogether. Satan has perfected the process in our culture by exploitation of the media. Sin is made to appear attractive, hip, and cool. For example, our culture continually trumpets that *casual sex is natural, everyone has needs, these are just innocent pleasures and personal weaknesses.* Think of how those in darkness promote homosexuality, abortion, destruction of the family, and the lack of personal responsibility. Every day we are bombarded with deceitful and vain words that are intended to manipulate godly people into surrender. Those who walk in the light need to recognize these things for what they are. The words aimed at us are *empty*. While they may sound smart and sophisticated, they ring with the sound of hollowness. They are words devoid of understanding and are untruth.

This is why Christians are warned about the company they keep. Because darkness is *militant*, we need to guard against being deceived, "bad company ruins good morals." 1 Corinthians 15.33. While we endeavor to be light inside a dark world, we need to draw clear lines of demarcation. Those who live on the slippery slope will eventually fall. Those who live right on the edge will eventually be pulled over to the other side. Who are your primary associates? What media do you consume? "Finally, brothers, whatever is true, whatever is honorable, whatever is just, whatever is pure, whatever is commendable, if there is any excellence, if there is anything worthy of praise, think about these things." Philippians 4.8.

Those Who Choose Darkness Hate the Light

In both testaments, we read of the active opposition to and persecution of those who walk in God's way. Those who choose darkness hate the light. And by doing so, they have chosen their own condemnation. Jesus said, "And this is the judgment: the light has come into the world, and people loved the darkness rather than the light because their works were evil. For everyone who does wicked things hates the light and does not come to the light, lest his works should be exposed.But whoever does what is true comes to the light, so that it may be clearly seen that his works have been carried out in God." John 3.19–21. For those who love sin and desire to hide in it, darkness is a desirable thing. They despise the openness of light. They have completely given their heart over to Satan.

As we examine this principle, we begin to better understand the motives and methods of the Jewish persecution and murder of Jesus. There are two groups of people who are unaware of the presence of light. Those who are blind and those who close their eyes so tightly — they refuse to see. Those who rejected Christ are in the latter group because they rejected Jesus' light. Once they consciously made the decision to close their eyes, there was no limit to how far they would go to eliminate Jesus. Notice Jesus' statement: "You are of your father the devil, and your will is to do your father's desires. He was a murderer from the beginning, and does not stand in the truth, because there is no truth in him. When he lies, he speaks out of his own character, for he is a liar and the father of lies." John 8.44. Those who have teamed with Satan are fully committed to carrying out his purposes. As time progressed, the methods and decisions of Jesus' opponents became more brazen—ultimately achieving their intended result—murder.

The same thing happens today. Those who have committed to Satan and his darkness will stop at nothing to try to eliminate any reference to the light. Think of the war on Christianity that is presently taking place inside our country. Any reference to God is met with hostility and must be removed at all costs. What was once obscure and done behind the scenes, now is right out in the open as the elements of darkness boldly operate in our society. This is not unprecedented. "For they cannot sleep unless they have done wrong; they are robbed of sleep unless they have made someone stumble. For they eat the bread of wickedness and drink the wine of violence. But the path of the righteous is like the light of dawn, which shines brighter and brighter until full day. The way of the wicked is like deep darkness; they do not know over what they stumble." Proverbs 4.16-19.

This is why darkness should scare us. No matter how we get there, the longer we stay the more comfortable it becomes. Darkness has a way of hardening our heart. "But exhort one another every day, as long as it is called 'today,' that none of you may be hardened by the the deceitfulness of sin." Hebrews 3.13.

Conclusion

Now almost one year removed from his sudden burst into fame, Ted Williams has drifted back into media obscurity. He was last seen at one of the *Occupy Wall Street* protests in New York and works out of his home in Dublin, Ohio—as a voice-over artist for a New England based cable network. While he works hard to overcome them, the demons of the past will continue to haunt him—working overtime to get him to surrender to his addiction.

His story is like ours. Like Ted, we fight back the darkness and battle the weakness of the flesh. While we don't know Ted's spiritual condition, we do know that the Christian is not alone in this epic struggle. Through the presence of the Spirit, we can win. We are not alone. Our God is with us all the way. "Who shall separate us from the love of Christ? Shall tribulation, or distress, or persecution, or famine, or nakedness, or danger, or sword? As it is written, 'For your sake we are being killed all the day long; we are regarded as sheep to be slaughtered.'"

"No, in all these things we are more than conquerors through him who loved us. For I am sure that neither death nor life, nor angels nor rulers, nor things present nor things to come, nor powers, nor height nor depth, nor anything else in all creation, will be able to separate us from the love of God in Christ Jesus our Lord." Romans 8.35–39.

For Thought and Reflection:

- What is the only way we can suffer spiritual defeat?

- What is so tempting about Satan's promise of "freedom"?

- Describe how Satan laid the trap to ensnare Eve.

- How did the flesh play a role in leading to Eve's sin?

- What are some examples of "empty words" we hear inside today's culture?

- How can we guard our self against "empty words?"

- Why do those who choose darkness hate the light?

- What should scare us most about darkness?

- Is there any hope for the hard hearted?

- What can we learn about our own struggles from Ted Williams?

The Character of Sin

Introduction:

For the last sixty years, our nation has found itself inside an immense struggle. Emanating from academia and Hollywood, ungodly forces have united to tear down traditional values and belief in God. Now, across every media platform, godly values and principles of right and wrong are openly and defiantly assailed. Atheists are prominently heralded as courageous heroes, [14] while those who stand for godly values are discredited. [15] From social media, to cable television, to print media, and network sitcoms, there is a constant drumbeat against those who hold to the values of traditional marriage, abstinence, pro-life, and belief in God.

Forty years ago, the hit network TV series *All in the Family* pioneered in setting a template that is still used today. The aim was to use humor with the fictional *Archie Bunker* to portray conservatives as foolish, intolerant, judgmental, and [16] racist. While Carroll O'Connor defended the show as only "joking" about these things, the rest is history. Now, that show looks tame, compared to the nightly lineup found on networks today. The limits are continually being pushed back. For example, here are the plot-lines of three popular sitcoms that have appeared during the fall of 2011:

- The November 8, 2011 episode of *Glee* called "The First Time," featured a homosexual couple struggling whether to "go all the way."

- The September 19, 2011 episode of *Two and a Half Men* featured jokes referencing prostitution, homosexuality, testicles, drunkenness and suicide. Characters say "b--ch," "a--," "freakin'" and misuse God's name.

- In the November 30, 2011 episode of *I Hate My Teenage Daughter*, conservative, Bible-based upbringing is mocked without respite. [17]

We have come a long, long way since *Leave it to Beaver* and *The Andy Griffith Show*. Many of us have personally watched the decline and feel powerless as things grow worse and worse.

As the assault on traditional values continues, and new generations come along, our country no longer sees the danger in sinful behavior. They do not realize there is a metaphorical pipeline of sewage just waiting to empty into their home through a computer, television screen, iPod, or e-reader. The stench and stain of ungodliness is just a mouse click, remote control button, or power switch away. The relentless and aggressive tactics of Satan and his forces have resulted in a moral implosion. What we've taken in through media over the last four decades is now reflected as the cultural norm. If history is any indicator, these things may very well contribute to the eventual destruction of everything Americans hold dear.

The darkness of a socially progressive culture has permeated in places where it would be least expected: inside our religious organizations. A large segment of church-going Americans are being lulled to sleep by a pseudo-gospel that is made up of nonjudgmental and soothing content that concentrates more on the physical than the spiritual. Many of the most liberal denominations have caved on the issue of homosexuality and abortion. With some segments of our religious culture—the only sin is to refer to sin as sin.

Sin is unpleasant to talk about. Many avoid it at all costs. While culture may have tried to rationalize it away, it is still there wreaking havoc in lives everywhere. Because sin is insidious and deadly, we must always be on watch. We must always be committed to decisively and swiftly deal with it, lest it take hold on our hearts. "Take care, brothers, lest there be in any of you an evil, unbelieving heart, leading you to fall away from the living God." Hebrews 3.12.

Seeing Sin For What It Is

Chrysostom once said, "I fear nothing but sin."[18] Sin is a blight on our world. In fact, it radically altered everything about God's creation. Sin brought with it pain, worry, sadness, fear, fighting, sickness and death. None of these were part of the world God created in Genesis 1-2. Can you imagine how Adam and Eve must have felt the first time they experienced these emotions and woke up with the first ache and pain? Can you feel their sadness as the animals they once could approach without fear now wanted to eat them? At every turn they would have been reminded of the cataclysmic effects of sin. The consequences of that first sin in the garden remain with us today. We live inside a world of sin and death and all kinds of hardships leading up to that death. With the exception of Enoch, Genesis 5.24, and Elijah, 2 Kings 2.11, every human being has died. James Gibbons has written, "This earth is a graveyard. And the hardships experienced in living are all part of the equation of death."[19] Concerning this Paul wrote: "the whole creation has been groaning together in the pains of childbirth until now." Romans 8.22. The pain of creation Paul mentions is described in detail in Genesis 3 after Satan's victory: "Cursed is the ground because of you; in pain you shall eat of it all the days of your life; thorns and thistles it shall bring forth for you; and you shall eat the plants of the field. By the sweat of your face you shall eat bread, till you return to the ground, for out of it you were taken; for you are dust, and to dust you shall return." Genesis 3.17b-19. **There is nothing joyous about sin.** John MacArthur has written, "Sin is the monarch of man. Sin is the lord of the soul. Sin is the king of humanity."[20] Sin devastates society. It is seen in every broken marriage and home, every wayward child, and every shattered friendship. It is behind prostitution, witchcraft, murder, theft, brokenheartedness, and unrelenting sorrow. God aptly described sin in Joshua 7.13. Here God calls it an "accursed thing."[21]

Scripture is not coy in its description of the devastation of sin. We read how:

- Sin stings, 1 Corinthians 15.55-56.

- Sin is an abomination, Proverbs 15.9; Jeremiah 44.4.

- Sin is filthy and polluted, Proverbs 30.12; Zechariah 3.3; 1 Kings 8.38; Isaiah 30.22.

- Sin is filled with iniquity, Isaiah 59.3, Psalm 90.8.

- Sin is evil, Matthew 15.19; Jeremiah 44.11.

- Sin is deceitful, Hebrews 3.13

- Sin is presumptuous, Proverbs 19.13.

- Sin brings death, Hebrews 9.27; Joshua 23.14; 1 Kings 2.2.

In scripture, sin is described as being extremely powerful, sinister, and dominating. If we are to be successful against it, we must have the courage to pull back the wrapping in which Satan has disguised sin. We must begin to see sin for what it is. In short, it is the sum of all bad things. It will destroy your life and your eternity. It is hideous, despicable, and base.

How the Bible Defines Sin

In three short words, God's word gives us a simple definition: "sin is lawlessness." 1 John 3.4. Later in the same epistle, the beloved apostle said, "all wrongdoing is sin." 1 John 5.17a. The first passage, 3:4, discusses the matter of sin in a positive manner (sin is a violation of a command of God). The second passage, 5:17, speaks of the matter in a negative manner (sin is a failure to keep or obey the commands of God). There are two other passages that set out to define sin. Paul wrote, "whoever has doubts is condemned" Romans 14.23, and James said "whoever knows the right thing to do and fails to do it, for him it is sin." James 4.17.

What law does sin violate? God's. His standard of righteous is the ultimate, inalterable way. His laws are based on what is right, holy, just, and good. God's way is the only way. As His creation, we are subject to it. Any violation of His law leads us into evil. It separates us from Him and makes us unholy.

As we try to wrap our mind around the deadly seriousness of sin, the Bible describes sin as rebellion. Think back to 1 John 3.4—*sin is lawlessness.* From almost the beginning, mankind has had a propensity to willingly transgress against God. In Leviticus 26.27, God described lawbreakers as those who *walk contrary to (Him).* When we sin, we move in opposition to God. One of the Hebrew words for sin is *Pasha,* which means to "trespass, apostatize, quarrel: offend, rebel, revolt, transgress."

Sin is a matter of the will. Think of the countless times God called a rebellious, idolatrous, and stubborn people to return. His people has been further described as belligerent and unbending. This is perfectly illustrated in Jeremiah 44, where God once again indicated His willingness to restore His relationship with them—if they would only turn to Him. To this Judah said, "As for the word that you have spoken to us in the name of the Lord, we will not listen to you." Jeremiah 44.16. God's people had become hardened to the point where nothing would prick through the callousness of their heart. They simply were not interested in anything God had to say. As we discussed in our previous lesson, this is one of the awful effects of sin—it hardens and causes one to only pursue darkness with an even greater hunger. Any thought of returning into the light is met with the strongest of resistance. They go on to say "we will do everything that we have vowed, make offering to the queen of heaven and pour out drink offerings to her, as we did, both we and our fathers, our kings and our officials, in the cities of Judah and in the streets of Jerusalem. For then we had plenty of food, and prospered, and saw no disaster." 44.17. The *queen of heaven,* was a name for Ishtar, the Mesopotamian goddess of love and fertility. Nothing, not even God Himself, could persuade the people to return to Him. Before we came to Christ, we rebelled against God. Paul writes, that we were once "alienated and hostile in mind, doing evil deeds." Colossians 1.21. We were in the midst of a very grave situation.

Sin is pictured as an incurable disease. Isaiah described the sin of his day in this way: "Ah, sinful nation, a people laden with iniquity, offspring of evildoers, children who deal corruptly! They have forsaken the Lord, they have despised the Holy One of Israel, they are utterly estranged." Isaiah 1.4. Isaiah continues by describing the people being full of sin—as a person who becomes full of disease: "The whole head is sick and the whole heart faint, From the sole of the foot even to the head, there is no soundness in it, but bruises and sores and raw wounds; they are not pressed out or bound up or softened with oil." 1.5b-6. God's people found themselves in a desperate situation. Sin had completely overtaken them and there was no way they could extricate it. The same is true for people of all time. The only cure for sin is to begin a relationship with the Great Physician, Luke 5.31.

If people really understood their plight, they would immediately seek a remedy. But darkness has a way of blinding individuals to the point that they cannot see anything—including what is right in front of them. And the longer a person stays in this situation the more comfortable it becomes. A few years ago I visited the home of a person who had fallen prey to a life altering illness. For years, she had raised chihuahuas and sold them to people in the community. As her health declined, the lady could no longer care for the eight dogs inside her home. When I came by for a visit, it was obvious the dogs had had free reign of the home for weeks. Feces and vomit were scattered throughout the home. Warm, humid weather with no air conditioning made matters worse. You could smell the inside of the home before you walked onto the porch. It was an awful experience. I couldn't leave fast enough, but as I was leaving—I was overtaken by an overwhelming sadness. This was not the way I had remembered this person from my youth. We may wonder how *any person* could ever live in such conditions—and the answer is simple—*you get used to it and no longer see things as they really are.* This same thing happens with those caught in sin. They have been blinded to the way things really are and cannot see they have been condemned to death by the most insidious disease known to mankind: sin.

Sin is Hard Work

In a sermon many years ago, John MacArthur made a powerful point concerning the great effort people make to engage in sin. It is worthy of our consideration. Jeremiah spoke of those who "weary themselves committing iniquity." Jeremiah 9.5. Sin isn't easy. We have to expend effort to do it. Despite the pain, it is amazing to see how hard people work at being sinners. It is expensive. It causes people to run around, stay up all night, carouse, get drunk, get high, get arrested, wreck their car, lose a wife, destroy a family, get sick, and go to the hospital.

Consider the story we find in Genesis 19. Angels came to visit Lot at Sodom. Sodom was one of the wickedest cities on earth—full of all sorts of debauchery and sexual perversion. When the angels arrive, Lot invites them to stay inside his house. He extends hospitality to them. Before retiring, the men of Sodom gathered outside Lot's home and demanded he send the angels outside so they could have sex with them. Lot refused. In fact, he offered his daughters to them. (This offer by Lot, shows he had become desensitized to sin.) The men outside refused and began to use violence to enter Lot's house to assault his two visitors. They were literally going to break down the door of the house. The angels struck the men with blindness, *but not even that* extinguished their illicit desires: "they wore themselves out groping for the door." 19.11.

We see similar examples of this throughout Scripture and even today:

* Psalm 7.14—In the years Saul pursued David, wishing to take his life, Cush served as Saul's agent—seeking David's life. David described him as being *pregnant with evil, conceives trouble, and gives birth to deceit.* No matter how difficult it was, or how much pain it caused him, Cush would not relent against David.

* Ezekiel 24.12—This passage is concerned with Jerusalem who had *wearied herself with toil, its abundant corrosion does not go out of it.* Jerusalem was so busy with sin, she had worn herself out with it.

- Proverbs 4.16—*For they cannot sleep unless they have done wrong; they are robbed of sleep unless they have made someone stumble.* It has been said, "Sin is hard work. People go to hell sweating."[22]

It Starts With Just One Sin

Paul wrote: "The wages of sin is death." Romans 6.23. In James 1 we read, "Then desire when it has conceived gives birth to sin, and sin when it is fully grown brings forth death." James 1.15. In both passages "sin" is used in singular form. In other words, **one** will bring about death. Going back to Genesis 2, God said that **the sin** of eating the forbidden fruit would bring about death. By one simple act, Adam and Eve willingly chose to give up what they had in the garden. Satan's methods have not changed and his deception is that effective. He constantly tells us, *it won't matter this one time,* and *no one will ever know.* One sin does matter, just ask Adam and Eve! One sin has the ability to separate us from our relationship with the Father.

With all seriousness, we must give attention to holiness and the need to walk in the light. Peter said, "prepare your minds for action, and being sober minded, set your hope fully on the grace that will be brought to you at the revelation of Jesus Christ. As obedient children do not be conformed to the passions of your former ignorance, but as he who called you is holy, you also be holy in all your conduct, since it is written, 'You shall be holy, for I am holy.'" 1 Peter 1.13-16.

Conclusion:

Our nation has long since crossed the line and fallen down a slippery slope. We have actually reached a point now where forty year old sitcoms like *All in the Family* look tame. What is truly scary is that our descent into the moral abyss will only gain speed as we travel through time. What future generations face may be unimaginable to those of us presently alive.

Can we turn things around? Certainly. With the power of God all things are possible. May we realize that change begins to happen when each person and each family determine to make God's way their way. Change will happen when we thoroughly acquaint ourselves with a true and accurate understanding of sin. Only when we see it in its true form will we be steadfast in making **every** effort to avoid it at every turn. "Since we have these promises, beloved, let us cleanse ourselves from every defilement of body and spirit, bringing holiness to completion in the fear of God." 2 Corinthians 7.1.

For Thought and Reflection:

- Describe the media influence on the morals of our nation.

- Why do so many avoid a discussion about sin at all costs?

- Who are the only two human beings who have never died?

- List eight ways the Bible describes sin. Discuss.

- In what four ways does the Bible define sin? Discuss.

- In what ways do you see similarities to Jeremiah 44 in today's culture?

- What is the only cure for sin?

- How does sin blind us to our surroundings?

- How is sin "hard work?"

- Do you feel there is any hope for our nation to "turn things around?" Why?

Conflicts Between Darkness and Light

Introduction

On a steamy August morning in 1974, Richard Nixon addressed the White House staff as he and his family prepared to board a westbound plane to California. This was no typical morning, however. In a nationally televised speech the night before, he announced his resignation as the President of the United States. A nation filled with shock and disbelief was glued to their televisions, as reporters covered the surreal events. Never before, had a sitting President resigned. As Nixon approached the podium, with his family standing behind him in support, heavy emotion filled the room. In a moving twenty-two minute speech, the formerly bold and confident leader, was now a broken man. A political career that had propelled him to serve as a United States Representative, Senator, Vice President for eight years, and now President for over five years had crashed into smoldering ruins. Driven by insecurity and distrust, Nixon's bad political decisions led to fatal errors, which then had to be concealed in a massive coverup. As investigators did their work, bringing to light what had been done in darkness, the undeniable truth presented itself. There was no way out. His time of reckoning had come. As Nixon reflected on his situation that morning, he said "Only if you have been in the deepest valley can you ever know how magnificent it is to be on the highest mountain." [23] Nixon died in 1994 and is still one of the most polarizing figures in American politics. While it can be argued whether Nixon was truly repentant for the misdeeds he committed while in office, no one can deny that darkness overruled him and it cost him everything.

Previously, we have discussed the constant conflict between spiritual light and darkness. Light represents God. Darkness represents evil. The work of God is diametrically opposed to the activity of Satan and his subordinates. Spiritual darkness is not passive. Its very nature is *militant* as it is actively promoted by Satan and his forces. We must understand the *ever present* danger of Satan's methods to penetrate our defense and use us as a pawn to advance his agenda. He does this through the hardening of our hearts. Satan influences us toward personal and active opposition to God's rule and truth. One of the strongest examples in the Old Testament of personal rebellion against God is seen in the actions of Israel's first king. Saul was God's chosen representative to lead Israel. After a flashy beginning, Saul quickly found himself on a downward descent, struggling with insecurity, selfish pride, and disenchantment from the people of Israel. After his disobedience led to God's decision to reject him, Saul's descent rapidly gained speed. When David comes on the scene, Saul's affection for him quickly turns into jealousy and rage which later morphed into hatred and attempted murder. Spiraling downward, Saul's life ended with a chain of events that resulted with his death at the hand of his own sword. His squandered talents and wasted opportunities are glaring examples of the deadly impact darkness can have on our physical and spiritual life.

Saul's lack of spiritual and national leadership left the nation in a depressing gloom. The nation craved genuine and bold leadership. David fit this need perfectly. "More than with any other person, Israel is fascinated by David, deeply attracted to him, bewildered by him, occasionally embarrassed by him, but never disowning him." [24] David gave the people someone to believe in and as time progressed it was clear to all that God was with him, 1 Samuel 18.14.

David is presented in dynamic contrast to Saul. David was "a man after God's own heart." Acts 13.22-24. He brought unparalleled success to Israel and set the example of glorifying God at every turn. His life of faith and humility serves as a blueprint for how we can withstand any incursion of darkness. While David's successes are numerous, his struggles and escapades into sin are notable. In later life, darkness severely impacted David's effectiveness as king. But yet, the majority of David's life can be characterized by his continual trust in the deliverance of God. David is distinguished from Saul in the way he depended on God and how he responded to God in turning from seasons of sin. Psalm 51 is a great example of David's sensitivity to sin. After being confronted by Nathan for his sin with Bathsheba and the murderous coverup, David opens his heart to God. "Create in me a clean heart, O God, and renew a right spirit within me. Cast me not away from your presence, and take not your Holy Spirit from me. Restore to me the joy of your salvation, and uphold me with a willing spirit. Then I will teach transgressors your ways, and sinners will return to you. Deliver me from bloodguiltiness, O God, O God of my salvation, and my tongue will sing aloud of your righteousness. O Lord, open my lips, and my mouth will declare your praise. For you will not delight in sacrifice, or I would give it; you will not be pleased with a burnt offering. The sacrifices of God are a broken spirit; a broken and contrite heart, O God, you will not despise." Psalm 51.10-17.

In this chapter we will examine Saul's continual conflict with darkness. How did it blind Saul from seeing the delivering power of God? How did Satan use Saul's personal insecurities as an entry point for pride and rebellion? What must we learn as we seek to overcome the incursions of darkness in our life?

Saul's Continual Conflict with Darkness:

Even with an early military victory over the Ammonites, Saul seemed to be an underachiever as king. This was not because he did not have every opportunity to excel. Saul had been *handpicked* by God. "God did not pick Saul to fail. God picked him because he had the potential to succeed. God would have made Saul's descendants a continuing dynasty over Israel."[25] Even though God had made it clear that He would stand behind Saul, he struggled with insecurity and this allowed spiritual darkness to go to work.

Because of his lack of faith in God, Saul's low sense of self worth and insecurity morphed into an acute case of self centeredness. **Saul could never break free of himself.** This *self-worship* led to Saul's undoing. He constantly felt the need to remind everyone around him that he was king. One example is seen in 1 Samuel 14.24 where Saul declared the Philistines as his personal enemy. This conflict was not about Saul—it was about God. Selfishness caused him to lose sight of the real purpose. The Philistines were the enemy of God, not Saul, 10.7-8. Darkness blinded him to what would have been a perfect opportunity to draw the attention of his ragtag band of soldiers to the delivering power of God. His men came into battle unskilled and woefully equipped, lining up against a Philistine force that was one of the most highly trained and heavily armored of its time. Excelling in metal-working, the Philistines used advanced weaponry and took over all the blacksmith shops in Israel, limiting the Israelites ability to produce swords and spears, 1 Samuel 13.19-22. Even though the circumstances looked bleak, Saul forgot that God was on their side and would provide a crushing victory. **Darkness hampers our ability to see past the obstacles and examine the guaranteed deliverance promised to those who trust in God.** Later in 1 Samuel 14, the chain of events that resulted from Saul's rash vow so diminished the spirit of his men that they walked away from an opportunity to pursue the fleeing enemy. In the span of just a few seconds and with a few short words, Saul's lack of faith cost his nation what could have been a decisive and permanent victory against Philistia. The reason for the missed opportunity can be placed only on one thing. Darkness.

After his victory over the Amalekites, Saul's self centeredness is seen again as he busied himself with setting up a monument to call attention to *his* victory, 1 Samuel 15.12. Why not a monument built to remember *God's* great victory? Darkness. The building up of his image as king was the foremost thing on his mind. It was all about Saul and *never* about God. This story teaches us an important lesson in that **sin is self motivated**. Satan is very successful in tempting us to believe that we are doing God's will, especially when we are more concerned about our own desires than God's purposes. Saul walked right into this trap and hardened his heart. If not dealt with decisively, darkness can cause our heart to harden like concrete. We see this process in vivid detail in how Saul reacted after David's victory over Goliath, 18.8-9. There was no room for anyone else on the stage. David **had** to be eliminated. **Nothing** else mattered. What propelled Saul down this path of bitterness, hatred, and murderous intent? Darkness.

Darkness influenced Saul to blame others in order to justify himself. In moments of crisis, Saul always placed his confidence in himself and not God. When confronted about his justification for offering a sacrifice rather than continuing to wait for Samuel, Saul was quick to point the blame somewhere else. In his mind, it was Samuel's fault. "The people were scattering from me, and you (Samuel) did not come within the days appointed, and the Philistines had mustered at Michmash." 1 Samuel 13.11. While we at first might be sympathetic to Saul's case, as his forces were deserting him in droves, a spiritual leader would have drawn the attention of the people to God. But yet, we see no reference to Saul's leadership in calling his troops to petition God in prayer. His faith went only as far as he could see. His confidence rested in his own military strength rather than divine action. It was not Samuel's fault that Saul failed the test. Saul's lack of spirituality caused him to fail the test and it cost him greatly. Because of his sin, God determined that his family would not be the ruling dynasty of Israel, 13.13-14. This pattern of shifting the blame continues in 1 Samuel 15. When confronted by Samuel, he twice blames his disobedience on the people, 15.15, 21. Did Saul fear the people more than God?

Fear caused Saul to take matters into his own hands. A prophet delayed? *I'll do it my way.* Kill every Amalekite and utterly destroy their spoil? *Don't bother me with the facts, I'll do it my way.* He based his actions on what seemed wise to him at the time—even in situations where God plainly revealed the specifics of what He wanted, 15.2-3. We can develop a stronger devotion to our own logic than the wishes of God. Blaming others can become nothing more than a cover for cold hearted rebellion. Time after time, Saul demonstrated a myopic and near-sighted determination to ignore God's expectations. Understand that **darkness takes away our respect for who God is.** What we want can become more important than anything. Where are your desires? How much do you respect God?

Finally, darkness led Saul to only have an *association* with God. While Saul believed in God and communicated with Him, he never built a *relationship* with God. Outwardly, all looked well. He was present at sacrifices to make fine speeches, he surrounded himself with priests, he used religious sounding words and tried to create and maintain an aura of personal piety and loyalty to God. But inwardly, he was very far from God. Saul wanted all the benefits God had to offer, but **refused to surrender to God.** "In every human interaction, there is an enormous difference between commitment to a relationship and commitment to an association. The most significant of human interactions always are devoted to a pursuit of and a maintenance of relationship. People committed to God always seek relationship, not mere association. The manner in which relationship and association react to the realities of personal insecurity are radically different." [26] Saul's bad decisions reflected his impetuous and self serving attitude. His efforts to free himself from the rule of God resulted in a far worse bondage to Satan, sin, and death.

David's life stands in great contrast to Saul's. In almost every situation, he looked for ways to exalt God. David was *God-centered.* Because he had a "relationship" with God, he was secure, humble, and dedicated to using every opportunity to honor God's greatness. David's viewpoint of God differed from Saul. In almost every instance, David reacted differently to life circumstances. This is because David kept an open heart and lived his life with humility. Even while caught up in the most awful of circumstances, when confronted directly with sin, David refused to blame someone else and took full responsibility for his actions. The contrast between Saul's response to Samuel in 1 Samuel 15 and David's response to Nathan in 2 Samuel 12 and Psalm 51 could not be greater.

How to Overcome the Incursions of Darkness

The problems that David and Solomon faced are no different today. In some way, Satan and his forces of darkness will use their influence to undermine your relationship with God. John said, "For all that is in the world—the desires of the flesh and the desires of the eyes and pride of life—is not from the Father but is from the world. And the world is passing away along with its desires, but whoever does the will of God abides forever." 1 John 2.16-17. Satan impacted both men in all three aspects and will do the same to us in ways that are unique to our individual circumstances and situation. How can we resist?

Understand your existence is about God—not your selfish ambitions. God determines your purposes, not your own personal desires. In day to day life, Paul successfully exemplified this, Galatians 2.20. Think of his willingness to walk away from a very prominent and lucrative position in Judaism to serve God. When reflecting on this he wrote, "But whatever gain I had, I counted as loss for the sake of Christ. Indeed, I count everything as loss because of the surpassing worth of knowing Christ Jesus my Lord. For his sake I have suffered the loss of all things and count them as rubbish, in order that I may gain Christ." Philippians 3.7-8. And I would be remiss if I did not mention the supreme example in Jesus who set aside His personal wishes in order to accomplish God's redeeming work of mankind, Luke 22.42; John 5.30; 6.38; 12.27; 17.1-3.

Never push God out of your life. David made some awful mistakes, lowering himself to commit adultery and murder. For over a year he hoped that the matter would just be swept under the rug, with no one ever knowing the depths of his sin. God was patient during this time, hoping David would turn on his own.

When he did not, Nathan delivered the difficult message. It was a message David needed to hear. He was convicted of his sin and turned back to God. Don't misunderstand just how important this time was in his life. For David, the easy thing would have been to push God out of the picture (like Cain and Saul did) and go his own way. But here, in the darkest of moments, David invites God back into his life. Even if you make disastrous mistakes, you can always come back to God. In this life, you can never drift outside of God's reach. "Consequently, he is able to save to the uttermost those who draw near to God through him, since he always lives to make intercession for them." Hebrews 7.25. Develop the kind of heart that is always ready to repent.

Accept responsibility for your choices—even the sinful ones. This is so difficult while living inside a culture that has diminished the idea of personal responsibility. If you are headed down the wrong road, stop living in denial. Quit lying to yourself. Don't shift the focus onto someone else. Stop moving away from God and turn around. Invite God into your life. Think of the beautiful story recorded in Luke 15. The prodigal son blew it. He could not have gone much farther into the mire. "But, *when he came to his senses,* he came home to the loving arms of his father who welcomed him as a forgiven son." Luke 15.11-24. Own up to your situation and come home. Let the loving arms of your eternal Father surround you and feel the warmth of His gracious touch.

Conclusion

In the American political scene, Richard Nixon's fall from grace could not have been greater. He will forever be associated with one of the most egregious abuses of power our nation has ever known. During the two decades after his presidency he dedicated his life to rehabilitating his image. But the consequences of his actions followed him wherever he went. Still to this day, the mention of his name stirs the emotion of every American who lived during that time. As we look at his failure, let us be impressed with the power of darkness and the hidden reality of brokenness and shame that comes along with it. When we go through seasons of disobedience and times of doubting God, let us realize the glory of being on the mountaintop with God and trust that through our humble and repentant heart, He will lead us home to eternal bliss in heaven.

For Thought and Reflection:

- In what ways did Saul worship himself?

- How does darkness hamper our ability to see past the obstacles of life?

- What pushed Saul down the path of bitterness and hatred?

- How does darkness take away our respect for God?

- Describe the difference between an "association" with God and a "relationship" with God.

- What are some key components in building a "relationship" with God?

- What are some ways we can keep a heart that is "ready to repent"?

- After succumbing to sin, what are some things Satan tells us about the reach of God?

How Darkness Affects Your Life

Introduction:

During the fall of 2000, the football world found itself in a buzz over Virginia Tech quarterback Michael Vick. His story was inspirational. Growing up in the Newport News, VA projects the young Vick turned to sports as an escape from the violence and drug abuse that surrounded his family and friends. Leaving his college career behind early for the NFL, Vick was the hottest candidate in the 2001 draft. He was chosen as the first overall pick, something never before achieved by an African American, and during his six year career in Atlanta, Vick led the Falcons to two playoff appearances. It was the ultimate American "rags to riches" story. Rewarded with a $130 million contract, the most lucrative in the NFL at the time, Vick was flying high. Surrounded by "friends" who promised to make him even more money by marketing his image, he spent lavishly and mingled with those of questionable reputation. As he developed his "bad boy" reputation, his years in Atlanta were not without controversy. But nothing could compare to the disgust and righteous anger of the nation when Vick was implicated and later arrested on federal dog fighting charges. On August 24, 2007 Vick pleaded guilty as charged. In his plea agreement, he admitted to being guilty in every respect: killing animals that wouldn't fight by beating, electrocuting, shooting, drowning, and hanging. Vick also admitted that it was largely his money (received in a signing bonus from the Falcons) that financed the illegal operation. While he awaited sentencing, Vick failed a random drug test. His employer sued to get back the signing bonus they gave him.

Vick's life was crumbling and he didn't seem to care. On December 10, 2007 Vick was sentenced to a 23 month stay in the federal prison in Leavenworth, KS. When Vick went to prison people cheered. In late 2007, perhaps no one was more disliked in America than Michael Vick. The most vocal of critics even called for his execution. [27]

Released in July 2009, Vick recounted what it was like inside prison walls. "The first day I walked into prison, and he slammed that door, I knew, you know, the magnitude of the decisions that I made, and the poor judgment, and what I, you know, allowed to happen to the animals. And, you know, it's no way of, you know, explaining, you know, the hurt and the guilt that I felt. And that was the reason I cried so many nights. And that put it all into perspective. [28] What I did, you know, being away from my family, letting so many people down. I let myself down, you know, not being out on the football field, being in a prison bed, in a prison bunk, writing letters home, you know. That wasn't my life. That wasn't the way that things was supposed to be. And all because of the so-called culture that I thought was right—that I thought it was cool. And I thought it was, you know, it was fun, and it was exciting at the time. It all led to me laying in a prison bunk by myself with no one to talk to but myself." When asked who was to blame for his actions, Vick squarely said, "I blame me." [29]

Vick didn't learn the magnitude of his transgressions until it was too late. Due to his poor judgment and arrogant attitude he lost almost everything. Recounting the way he lived before his conviction, Vick said his life would not have changed without being caught. He ignored repeated warnings of his mother, saying her words went "in one ear and out the other." "The best thing for me, that ever happened to me up to this point, as crazy as it may sound, was me being shipped off to Kansas. Because other than that, I wasn't going to change. I wasn't going to get all the people away from me that was leeches and wanted to be around. I wasn't going to stop fighting dogs. There was nothing nobody could have done to change my situation but the man upstairs, who said, 'Listen, before this goes any further, I'm going to take all this away from you for a while.'" [30]

Darkness most certainly has its affects. While we may have never heard the cold metal clang of a prison door close behind us, we all know what it is like to be in bondage to sin. When we fall prey to sin's enticement, at first things are good. Sin is fun and exciting. It is in vogue and edgy. It promises to be fulfilling and enrich us. *It just feels right.* Then, the thrill begins to fade or the law comes calling. When it has finally finished its course, we are left alone to deal with the consequences. Now the shame, guilt, and remorse weigh down on us. Reality presents itself and we see our sin for the raw sewage it is. It is truly an awful moment when we face the fact that Satan has left us trapped inside, miserable, cold and alone.

These are critical moments. In the darkest and most desperate of situations, we each have a decision to make. How we react depends on our willingness to resist Satan. The *easy* thing would be to give up, push God out of the picture (like Cain and Saul did), and go our own way. Some choose to walk down this path, deluded by the lie that it would be better to trade the *temporary* pain of embarrassment for the *continual* pain that comes with unconfessed sin. In these pivotal moments, the *harder* thing to do is choose a better path. Will we swallow our pride and invite God back into our life? Will we admit our sin? When we make disastrous mistakes, we can always come back to God. "Consequently, he is able to save to the uttermost those who draw near to God, since he always lives to make intercession for them, Hebrews." 7.25. See also Luke 15.11-24.

How does darkness affect us? How can we overcome and find victory?

Darkness capitalizes on the embarrassing aspects of sin.

There is a deep psychological affect associated with holding things in. After his sin with Bathsheba and subsequent coverup by killing Uriah, David found himself in agony and emotional distress. He was physically ill and mentally disturbed. The last thing he wanted was to have his adultery and murderous actions exposed. By covering his sin, David knowingly handed over control of his life to Satan. While he may have tried to justify himself, he was dying inside. *Well, I may not be perfect, but at least I'm not like* _____. Or, *other than this, look at all the good I've done for God.* Justification, rationalization, and comparison are all tools we use to sugar coat the poison Satan feeds us after he has us inside his trap.

Struggling and writhing in the pain of remorse, David's failure to confess his sin was devastating. "For when I kept silent, my bones wasted away through my groaning all day long. For day and night your hand was heavy upon me; my strength was dried up as by the heat of summer." Psalm 32.3-4. "O LORD, rebuke me not in your anger, nor discipline me in your wrath For your arrows have sunk into me, and your hand has come down on me. There is no soundness in my flesh because of your indignation; there is no health in my bones because of my sin. For my iniquities have gone over my head; like a heavy burden, they are too heavy for me. My wounds stink and fester because of my foolishness, I am utterly bowed down and prostrate; all the day I go about mourning. For my sides are filled with burning, and there is no soundness in my flesh. I am feeble and crushed; I groan because of the tumult of my heart." Psalms 38.1–8. David also said: "For I know my transgressions, and my sin is ever before me. Against you, you only, have I sinned and done what is evil in your sight, so that you may be justified in your words and blameless in your judgment." Psalm 51.3-4. Other passages noting David's attitude when struggling with his sin are found in Psalm 40.12 and 41.4. Concealed sin is like a cancer—it eats away and destroys us from within. Until David found the courage to deal with his sin, his life was slowly draining away. Imagine the scene. Here is the great king of Israel now living in the shadows of his own palace. Because of his direct disobedience to God, sin had shriveled him into something he was never destined to be.

Embarrassment and shame are God given emotions to push us toward repentance. But like every other thing, Satan has a way of twisting these emotions into something God never desired. In order to entice us to cover our sin, Satan exploits our personal pride and discourages us from admitting our sin to *anyone.* **Satan uses fear to keep us inside his trap.** In essence, our pride and stubbornness are turned into our own personal prison. *What if someone else finds out? What will they think of me? I'll lose my position and influence. I could lose my family and my job.* And Satan's list goes on and on. If Satan succeeds in scaring us with these unknowns, he will bury us even deeper in sin. How? Consider how we quickly want to cover or deny our faults and failures. Sin moves us into "react" mode. We cover up, smear over, and scheme until we find ourselves lost inside a maze we can never escape. This downward spiral always starts with silence. One writer has said, "Silence always leads to more pain and guilt festering inside. It always corrodes away our soul. It corrodes away our spirit, and it always, always, always begins to affect other parts of our lives." [31] Today, so many are struggling with family issues, compulsive habits, and sexual addiction. They want out. Fear holds them back. Lying there in misery, Satan says that silence is the best way to handle it.

But that's simply another lie. Covering our sin and living in denial is extremely hard work. It only leads to more sin. If we make the choice to believe Satan, sin continues to pile up and the consequences become more devastating. Our spouse, children, co-workers, church, and family, can all be made to suffer from our indiscretions. In the Old Testament we read how Achan's indiscretion resulted in his entire family being executed along with him, Joshua 6-7. If you are caught in the trap of sin, the best course of action is to stop flailing around, which only adds to your pain. Quit digging deeper the hole you're in. Stop before you hurt yourself more, bury yourself deeper, and hurt those around you. In this life, you are never too far away for God's rescue.

The Liberating Power of Confession.

"Whoever conceals his transgressions will not prosper, but he who confesses and forsakes them will obtain mercy." Proverbs 28.13. If you've been trapped by Satan's snare, there is absolutely no way you can release yourself. You cannot undo what has been done. **The first step in being extricated from the situation is admitting there is a problem.** There will be no success until there is a reckoning with yourself concerning the reality of the situation. Isn't this what the prodigal son did? "How many of my father's hired servants have more than enough bread, but I perish here with hunger." Luke 15.17b. This was the painful truth. Someone has said, "Blessed are those who know they are in trouble and have sense enough to admit it." [32] The first step in being released from the prison of pride is to admit failure.

Once personal realization and admission for the problem has occurred, the next step is to take the matter before God, Luke 15.18. We must be willing to **admit our spiritual poverty.** We come to God deeply stained with sin. David said, "create in me a clean heart, O God" Psalm 51.10. Psalm 51 is amazingly powerful. Imagine the scene. Here is David, the great and mighty king, approaching God as a humble beggar, pleading for mercy. All of David's defenses had been lowered. All responsibility had been assumed. There was no denying and no blame-shifting. His words are full of simple honesty. They are:

Emphatic: *I have sinned, 51.4.*

Specific: *Deliver me from bloodguiltiness, 51.14.*

Frank: *(I have) done what is evil in your sight, 51.4.*

Directed to God: *51.1, 10, 14-15.*

Seeking God's forgiveness: *51.7, 10-11.* [33]

Paul wrote, "Blessed are those whose lawless deeds are forgiven, and whose sins are covered; blessed is the man against whom the Lord will not count his sin." Romans 4.7-8. There is a purpose in taking the matter before God. The aim of confession is not to erase or ignore the consequences of sin, it is to restore joy. This was David's desire: "Let me hear joy and gladness; let the bones that you have broken rejoice, and Restore to me the joy of your salvation, and uphold me with a willing spirit." Psalm 51.8, 12.

"Secret sin, buried in the past, disturbs the present. Confessed sin, exhumed from the past, brings peace to the present. This is what David learned, and, with God's help, this is what we will learn as well." [34]

When we get the matter in the open before God, we find immediate relief. "If we say we have no sin, we deceive ourselves, and the truth is not in us. If we confess our sins, he is faithful and just to forgive us our sins and to cleanse us from all unrighteousness." 1 John 1.8-9. Trust in the fact that God receives every broken heart. Let your contrition move you to confession and the amendment of your life. "Confession isn't doing something about our sin; rather, it means admitting that we can't do anything about our sin. It's admitting we need a Savior. We need what only Jesus can bring us, which is healing."

God's Blueprint for Building Togetherness in the Spiritual Family

"Therefore, confess your sins to one another and pray for one another, that you may be healed. The prayer of a righteous person has great power as it is working." James 5.16. The final section of James' epistle contains God's blueprint for what is to take place inside each local family of believers. It could be summarized as an atmosphere of close knit *togetherness*, where each other's lives were shared openly. These verses describe in detail what Paul must have meant by calling Christians to "rejoice with those who rejoice, weep with those who weep, and live in harmony with each other." Romans 12.15-16a. They are also an application of the principle Paul communicated in Galatians 6.1-2: "Brothers, if anyone is caught in any transgression, you who are spiritual should restore him in a spirit of gentleness. Keep watch on yourself, lest you too be tempted. Bear one another's burdens, and so fulfill the law of Christ."

James instructed those who were:

Suffering — *to seek prayer, 5.13a.*

Cheerful — *to sing praises, 5.13b.*

Sick — *to call on the Shepherds for anointing, 5.14.*

Caught in sin — *to confess, so that you may be healed, 5.16a.*

These activities were to be done with a specific purpose in mind. By alerting others of their physical and spiritual ailments, each Christian could count on the help and encouragement of their brothers and sisters. Christians have been instructed to pray for each other. **It is hard to know what to pray for if the specifics are not communicated.** Confession aids the sense of *togetherness* inside the local church. It reminds the Christian that they are not alone in their struggles. We all cope with the weakness of the flesh. We all fall prey to Satan's devices. We all have a story to tell. This sense of brotherhood helps us grow stronger with each other and for the future. Together we affirm our faith and trust in God. Has today's church grasped the intention of the Holy Spirit? Are we truly committed to building this type of atmosphere?

What Keeps Us From Confessing Our Sins Before Others?

Most Christians would agree that there is much work to be done in order to build the type of close-knit togetherness mentioned in James 5.13-16. Each member of the congregation has a mutual responsibility in this area. This does not just fall on the Shepherds or Minister. Paul wrote, "We are to grow up in every way into him who is the head, into Christ, from whom the whole body, joined and held together by every joint with which it is equipped, when each part is working properly, makes the body grow so that it builds itself up in love." Ephesians 4.15b-16. *Everyone* can be filled with more compassion, love, and tenderness. *Everyone* can encourage and lift up those who are struggling. It doesn't have to be a large endeavor. A simple, *I'm praying for you,* or taking the time to *listen* to someone pour out their heart with a nonjudgmental response should be a goal for every Christian. What holds us back from following through? There are several factors.

Some Christians have little sense of togetherness or identification with each other as spiritual brothers and sisters. The most association they have with fellow Christians is 2-3 hours per week inside the confines of a church building. Think of the setting for a moment. Everyone gathers together a few minutes before the appointed time, dressed in their best and giving the appearance that they're problem free. After a quick few moments of small talk, all the correct religious procedures are conducted, and a message of strict adherence to a *religious system* is preached. Then, after a few more moments of small talk and visiting, members go home and for another week fend for themselves with little or no connection to those inside the church. There's little chance for healing and encouragement for any wounds that come along. While this may sound cynical, it is an unfortunate reality that exists in some places.

Another problem can be created when the teaching emphasis focuses more on *performance* than *relationship* with God. Instead of personal transformation, *performance* concentrates more on external actions. This can generate a toxic atmosphere inside a church family: one void of mutual love, compassion and vulnerability. It results in the breakdown of the principle in Galatians 6.2. The constant drive toward congregational purity leads to a fear of failure that causes individuals to wear a mask, pretending that they've got it all together spiritually. An unhealthy competition is created where individuals compare their righteousness to each other, instead of Christ. This goes against the principle in Ephesians 4.13: "until we all attain to the unity of the faith and of the knowledge of the Son of God, to mature manhood, *to the measure of the stature of the fullness of Christ.*" Constant biting and devouring causes spiritual families to be torn apart through personal criticism, gossip, comparative righteousness, and *expectation of the worst.*

Consider also the formalized process that has evolved in the church that says in order to be forgiven a person must go before the church and list out all of his or her sins. While *going forward* is certainly not outside the realm of expediency, care must be exercised in how this practice is employed. Spiritually immature individuals can abuse it by viewing the occasion as an opportunity to drag a person's wrongdoing out into the limelight. All sensitivity toward the one seeking to make their life right is disregarded. This is a direct result of a *performance based* approach to spirituality. It goes far beyond the intention of the apostolic writers.

Such circumstances break down the willingness of a person to share their struggles with those who should be the first to help and encourage. No wonder so many are hurting inside our church families! In the church, if we are to change the sterile atmosphere that discourages the practice of James 5.16, we must cease personal criticism of the person in sin. **Criticism does not take away sin.** Love, encouragement, and instruction motivate a person to get their sin problem out in the open so it can be handed over to the healing power of Almighty God.

When a local church family relates to God as Father, there is a growing a spirit of love, accountability, and gentle nurturing that is conducive to spiritual transformation. Because of their *relationship* with God, mature Christians understand the need to pick people up from their sin, Galatians 6.1. This stands strongly opposed to the law based spirit that enforces such high standards that people are forced to work overtime to keep from falling down. One spirit is encouraging. The other is rooted in fear. One spirit builds up. The other tears down.

Conclusion

Now having completed two seasons for the Philadelphia Eagles, Michael Vick is making progress down the long road of recovery. He credits his reformation to his new found relationship with God and the mentoring of Tony Dungy, former coach of the Indianapolis Colts who serves as his moral and spiritual leader. Vick's is, perhaps, one of the greatest stories of redemption of our time. He is scheduled to go off probation in May 2012 and was recently quoted, "I forget I'm on probation, because I live my life right and I don't do anything crazy no more."[35] And at least publicly, Vick has appeared to have learned his lesson. He has left old friends behind and is now an advocate for the humane treatment of animals. He has a long way to go. He may never live down his critics. But, he is headed in the right direction.

Before criticizing others who have been caught inside the trap of sin, remember one thing. **You are them.** While you may not have committed the same act they have, you have done some atrocious things before God. Let this realization drive you to a sense of humility. Let it cause you to move with grace and mercy toward others you interact with. Only these spiritual virtues can neutralize the effects of sin.

For Thought and Reflection

- Describe your emotions in the moments after you have realized the gravity of your sin.

- Why is your decision on how to react in these moments so critical?

- How do justification, rationalization, and compassion hold us in Satan's trap?

- What is God's purpose for shame and embarrassment?

- How does Satan twist our emotions when we are caught in sin?

- How is covering sin and living in denial hard work?

- What is the first step we must take in order to be released from sin?

- What is the purpose for confession?

- What is the principle communicated in James 5.13-16; Galatians 6.1-2; and Romans 12.15-16a?

- Why do spiritual families struggle with the application of these principles?

- How does a "works based" mindset shut down confession?

- Why is a critical atmosphere so toxic to a local church family?

How Does Law Relate to Darkness?

Introduction

During the late 1990s my family moved to South Dakota. We were immediately impressed with its governor, Bill Janklow. No matter the political persuasion, just about everyone could agree that he demonstrated his hands-on leadership with great passion. *Everyone* had an opinion on him. Usually it was one of two reactions: *love or hate.* This was not necessarily split down party lines. Getting his political start after serving as a lawyer who upheld the legal rights of poverty stricken Sioux Indians on the reservations, Janklow first served as state Attorney General, then as Governor for two eight year terms, 1979-1987 and 1995-2003. His persona fit very well into the rugged and brash, self reliant style that characterizes so much of the American West.

During the summer of 2000, forest fires decimated over 83,000 acres of the Black Hills National Forest. Spring blizzards that season dumped heavy wet snow on the forest, which took down many trees. As summer came on, the southern hills were hit with a severe drought, turning the downed timber into a tinderbox. On a Thursday afternoon in late August an arsonist started a fire on federal land just west of Jewel Cave. Initially, the National Park Service did little to slow down the fire. For the first few hours, they allowed the fire to burn through an area of diseased trees thinking they could save the time and money that would be expended later to cut down this section of forest. Then, without warning, the weather changed and the fire exploded. Hot, dry winds with extremely low humidity led to fire conditions unlike anything before in the recorded history of the area. Later, the Forest Service would say that on the first day, the inferno consumed "an average of about seven football fields of forest per minute."⊠36 Fifty miles away in Rapid City, smoke dominated the sky for days with the fire becoming so large that it created its own weather. All of this was going on with what seemed like a lethargic response from Forest Service. The frustration of local residents grew almost as fast as the fire. Finally, the governor stepped in. Flying out from Pierre to assess the situation personally, he pressed the Federal Government to step up their efforts. Janklow brought in every state asset possible to help suppress the fire and used his clout to cut through the red-tape of the federal bureaucracy to meet urgent needs. After 16 days, the Jasper fire was contained.

Because of his strong leadership, I'm sure if a poll had been taken in the months after the fire was extinguished the governor would have had an almost 100% approval rating in the Black Hills region. After completing a second eight year stint as governor in 2003, Bill Janklow decided to run for South Dakota's lone Congressional seat. He was easily elected. Janklow was on a roll. Wildly popular, it seemed that he couldn't lose.

But, the governor had a very bad reputation for ignoring the state speed limits. "South Dakotans who had never met or seen the governor knew Bill Janklow was a speeder. He had received a dozen speeding tickets and had been involved in a half-dozen accidents. Part of it was functional. He had a lot of ground to cover between church suppers and county fairs. Part was political. Speed seemed to be Janklow's trademark."[37] He even appeared to be very proud of his bad habit. During his state of the state message in 1999, Janklow argued for stiffer criminal penalties, and used himself as an example of why stiff penalties deter criminals. "Bill Janklow speeds when he drives. He shouldn't, but he does. And when he gets a ticket he pays it. If someone told me I was going to jail for two days for speeding, my driving habits would change. I can pay the ticket but I don't want to go to jail"[38].

Tragically, Janklow's words came back to haunt him in August 2003 when he sped down an eastern South Dakota gravel road at over 70 miles per hour. As he approached an intersection he ran the stop sign and crashed into motorcyclist Randy Scott, who was killed instantly. Janklow was charged with manslaughter and later found guilty. He was forced to resign from Congress in disgrace and serve 100 days in jail. He lost his law license for 2 years. Janklow, who had built a career as the South Dakota's chief law enforcement officer and furthered that career through enabling tough criminal standards as governor, had his political life snuffed out by his own willful violation of the law. I believe it would be easy to say Bill Janklow was severely flawed. While he did much good, the consequences of his ignoring certain and important aspects of the law will never be forgotten. There will always be an asterisk by his name.

What is our opinion toward "law?" How does darkness work through "law" to promote its purposes?

Paul's Remarks on the Law

"Law" is still a hotly contested topic in the church today, especially when taken into consideration on the topic of "grace." Perhaps there is no faster way to start a spirited and emotional discussion than to bring this subject up. Mention that "salvation is by grace through faith" Ephesians 2.8, and someone will quickly point out how "faith without works is dead." James 2.24-26. Speak of the need to "work out your own salvation with fear and trembling" Philippians 2.12, and you may quickly hear someone else quote Romans 4.5-6: "to the one who does not work but believes in him who justifies the ungodly, his faith is counted as righteousness, ...**God counts righteousness apart from works.**" No matter which perspective we come from, we must remember that truth is found in all of these Scriptures. Each individual has a personal responsibility to let the whole record speak for itself. Emphasizing some passages and ignoring others is not an honest approach to Bible study. Sometimes it can get very discouraging as well intentioned brethren talk past each other, arguing from their preconceived conclusions rather than carefully examining the Biblical record. Will we let scripture speak for itself and form our conclusions from there?

Paul extensively discussed these matters with his spiritual brothers and sisters in Rome. In his letter to them, Paul vigorously defended the biblical doctrine of salvation by faith apart from works of Law. This is the primary message of chapters 3-5. Our salvation is only possible through the precious gift of Jesus, who took our punishment and died on the cross in our place. Those in Christ have been "justified by his grace as a gift, through the redemption that is in Christ Jesus, whom God put forward as a propitiation by his blood, to be received by faith. This was to show God's righteousness, because in his divine forbearance he had passed over former sins. It was to show his righteousness at the present time, so that he might be just and the justifier of the one who has faith in Jesus." Romans 3.24-26. Adding what might be an exclamation point to an already powerful statement Paul says, "For we hold that one is justified by faith apart from works of the law." 3.28. These facts should come as a great relief to every Christian. Justification on the basis of law requires that it be kept perfectly in order to be free of guilt. No man has ever kept it perfectly, Galatians 3.8-10. If we did, we would have reason to boast, Romans 4.2.

Paul knew this would generate a strong reaction from his critics. Anticipating their charge that he was giving Christians a license to sin, he says "What shall we say then? Are we to continue in sin that grace may abound? By no means! How can we who died to sin still live in it." Romans 6.1-2. From there to the end of the chapter we find an eloquent and passionate defense of the doctrine of grace. **Where would we be without the grace of God?** When we realize just how marvelous this grace is, our hearts will be moved to follow through in surrender to His will. Who could *not* love God when they begin to comprehend the lengths God went to in order to rescue them from sin? It is our love and appreciation for God that fuels our faith. "If you love Me, you will keep My commandments." John 14.15. The only acceptable obedience is that which is in loving response to the mercy of our great God and eternal Father. Salvation is not on the basis of our action, but God's action.

To emphasize his point about salvation by grace through faith, Paul squarely addresses the inability of law to save.

- **3.20-21**—knowledge of sin comes through the law. The righteousness of God is manifested apart from the law.

- **3.28**—justification happens apart from works of the law.

- **4.13-14**—if those of law are heirs, then faith is void and the promise is nullified.

- **5.20**—the law came in to increase the trespass.

- **6.14**—we are no longer under law—but grace.

- **7.4**—in order to be joined to Christ, we must die to the law.

- **7.5**—law arouses sinful desires.

- **7.6**—Christians have been released from the law—having died to it.

It is hard to understand the earthquake Paul's writing would have caused inside the minds of Jewish readers. Most would have been shaken to the core. Their natural reaction would have been to charge Paul with disregarding law. It is the same today. Those who attempt to base their relationship with God on the number of commands they keep often make the same accusation. What they fail to realize is the fact that **no law,** old testament or new, **saves.** Salvation **is not** based on law, **period.** "If a law had been given that could give life, then righteousness would indeed be by the law." Galatians 3.21.

Now back to Romans. In 7.7-13, we find a detailed response to the anticipated objections of those who attempt to serve God on the basis of law. Was Paul disregarding law? Are Christians free to live absolutely anyway they please? **Absolutely not.** Even though justification is not found through law, concerning it Paul says:

- **7.7a**—the law is not sin.

- **7.7b**—the law identifies sin. It shows sin for what it really is.

- **7.12**—the law is holy and the commandments are holy, righteous, and good.

From what perspective should we view law? And what does this have to do with darkness?

"Law" Serves an Important Purpose

"Law" exists and there is a very distinct purpose for it. By revealing His will through His Word, God manifested it. His thoughts are clear. His expectations are just. They have been given for our good. We must respond with respect and reverence. "The Lord is in His holy temple; let all the earth keep silence before Him." Habakkuk 2.20. God does the talking. He is in charge and in control. We are expected to understand and comply with His wishes. "Walk as children of light and try to discern what is pleasing to the Lord,....Do not be foolish, but understand what the will of the Lord is." Ephesians 5.8b, 10, 17. God's Word is the **unalterable** standard. We have no right to change or modify it, Revelation 22.18-19.

Any decision we make to disregard God and His law is sin. "Sin is lawlessness." 1 John 3.4. "All wrongdoing is sin." 1 John 5.17. "The revealed will of God, creates the foundation for lawbreaking and guilt, law-keeping and righteousness, and court and judge, and justification and condemnation. All of these great things rest on this one assumption: 'there is law.'" "(If there were) no law there would be no law breaking. If there were no lawbreaking there would be no guilt. If there were no guilt, there would be no court. If there were no court, there would be no judge. If there were no judge, there would be no justification and no need for incarnation or crucifixion. The whole reality and the whole glory of redemption hang on the existence and excellence of law."[39]

In and of itself, law serves a very important purpose. **It is light.** "Your word is a lamp to my feet and a light to my path." Psalm 119.105. It defines the standard for righteousness. By defining righteousness, **it exposes sin.** It identifies our imperfections, flaws, and the weaknesses of the flesh. **The law fixes boundaries to our desires.** It teaches us what is *really* right and what is *really* wrong. It shows us where "lawful indulgences end and where sin begins." [40] Its precepts serve as guard posts in order to **protect us from eternal death.**

To back up his point, Paul uses the tenth commandment as an example, Romans 7.7b. Why covetousness? The root word "covet," simply means *desire*. Not all desires are sinful. However, *covetousness* describes desires that go beyond God's expectations. *Covetousness* hits at the illicit desires of the heart. Holding onto yearnings for things that are not proper is a violation of God's law. Paul says he would not have known covetousness was sin had the law not said so. In and of ourselves, we cannot see sin for what it is. "Sin is imperceptible as *sin*, before the law calls it sin by prohibiting it." [41]

Our desires are not the standard. *We* are not the judge of what is right or wrong. God's law is higher because it originates from God's perfection. God's law tells us what is right and wrong, good and bad, true and false. Think of how this contradicts the way of the world. Darkness says *we* should get what *we* deserve. What we *want* is our *right*. This is the same tactic Satan has been using since the garden, Genesis 3.5-6. Darkness pushes us to ignore God's influence in our life and decide for ourselves as to what is right and wrong. *Self* becomes the god that knocks the one, true God off the throne of our heart.

May we always understand that "law" is good. It is *not* our enemy. We must always possess the type of heart that humbly submits to God out of reverence and respect.

Sin is the Problem

"Law" is not our enemy, **sin** is. Darkness is so insidious that it can even work through something intended for our good to cause us to commit more sin. Paul said, "But *sin,* seizing an opportunity through the commandment, *produced in me all kinds of covetousness.* For apart from the law, sin lies dead." Romans 7.8. Verse 11 is very similar: "For *sin,* seizing an opportunity through the commandment, *deceived me and through it killed me.*" Darkness looks for every opportunity, **even going so far as God's law,** to produce sin in us.

God revealed His will for our ultimate benefit and protection. Remember Romans 7.12: "The law is holy, and the commandment is holy and righteous and good. In another place, it has been likened to a sharp sword. The word of God is living and active, sharper than any two-edged sword, piercing to the division of soul and of spirit, of joints and of marrow, and discerning the thoughts and intentions of the heart" Hebrews 4.12. God's word has the power to cut away the cancer of sin that invades our life. But, darkness uses what was intended for life and happiness against us. It takes the sword (God's word) and kills us. "The very commandment that promised life proved to be death to me." Romans 7.10.

How does darkness work through the commandment to kill us spiritually? Ultimately, "darkness *deceives* us." 7.11. Satan "is a liar and the Father of lies." John 8.44. He works through human logic. He works through our fleshly desires, making promises that he never intends to keep. But again we ask, how does Satan work through God's law to deceive us? There are two ways.

First, consider what darkness says when we read some of God's expectations that cover areas we are easily susceptible to because of the weakness of the flesh. Darkness whispers in the background saying "there's no way you can do that, and why would you want to anyway?" Darkness says, "you'll never match up." It says, "the standard is too high," and "it's not worth it, just give up, and enjoy the pleasures of the flesh."

Second, consider what darkness says when we examine the aspects of the law that come easy to us. We hear, "You're good at that. You've got no problems here. So prove to yourself and everybody else how strong *you* are." Darkness says "Take comfort in *your* righteousness and compare it to the shortcomings of those around you." Satan works in such a way that we choose to ignore simple, but powerful passages like, "Therefore let anyone who thinks that he stands take heed lest he fall." 1 Corinthians 10.12.

This is why it is so important to see darkness for what it *really* is. It offers *hopelessness* which can be relieved through **self indulgence,** or it offers *hopefulness* through **self righteousness.** This is deception through and through. As fast as we can, we must run from both perspectives. [42]

God's Law is What Matters. Not Ours.

Previously, we touched on the problem of self exaltation. A challenge for *every* New Testament Christian is the realization of the difference between "law" and "our law." We constantly fight the urge to take God's law and place our own individual slant on what God has revealed. This is usually done to benefit ourselves in some way. Darkness may influence us to loosen God's standards for ourselves while making them more stringent for those around us. Some have the tendency to make their own standards so strict and unyielding (all in the name of God) that it is impossible to live by.

Allegiance to our own standards can become so important to us that we use "our law" to judge the spirituality of others. The elevation of our own opinions is nothing more than **extending God's law.** When this happens, there can be a great temptation to enforce our own human judgments on everyone else. This is self-exaltation at its core and it is **darkness at work.**

For example, God has clearly communicated His principles on the attitude His sons and daughters need to have concerning their attire. The practice of *licentiousness* or *lasciviousness* is against God's law, Galatians 5.19-21, Jude 4. These words come from the same Greek word which is defined by "sensuality," "wanton acts or manners," "unbridled lusts," "outrageousness or shamelessness." The avoidance of any of these attitudes and actions should be the first priority for the Christian. These principles must be applied in the places we go, the way we dress, and how we behave around those of the opposite sex. The teaching of these **principles** should be our first priority. But if we are not careful, we can shift the focus from **principles** to **externals** and from **principles** to **specifics.** How many congregations are almost torn apart over wearing shorts or certain clothing that *may* or *may not* be modest— *depending on a person's judgment?* There aren't any specifics. There is a reason for that. God wants each individual to think and wrestle with this. God wants a response in faith that originates from the heart. Our personal conclusions should not be used as the standard to judge the spirituality of someone else. Some are so obnoxious that they actually become a source of discouragement to others, especially with new Christians and young people.

God's principles and expectations have been given to encourage us, as well as protect us. *This* is what really matters—not our own personal opinions or conclusions.

Conclusion:

Even after his own actions brought about the destruction of his political career and led to the death of an innocent individual, Bill Janklow still ignored the law. Once he was allowed to drive again, he accumulated at least four additional speeding tickets between 2008 and 2011. [43] The former South Dakota governor died on January 12, 2012 after battling brain cancer. He was 72.

May we endeavor to build our respect for God's law. It was given to help us by illuminating the pathway of righteousness. And as we live by it, let us live by faith and trust in God and not depend on our own flawed application of its principles and commands.

For Thought and Reflection:

- What kind of reaction would Paul's comments concerning the law in Romans 3-7.6 have generated among many Jews?

- What is the purpose of "law"?

- What do we need to know about our own desires?

- What is at the root of how darkness works? See John 8.44.

- How does darkness work through the law in order to kill us spiritually?

- How does the failure to distinguish the difference between "law" and "our law" lead to problems inside the church?

- What is so dangerous about equating our own standards with the standard God has set?

- Besides the subject of modesty, can you think of any other examples where individuals tend to equate their own judgments with "law"?

- Why do you think God would leave out "specifics" in the application of certain principles?

- For what purpose has God's commands and principles been given to us?

Understanding the Darkness of Calvary

Introduction

In the spring of 1945, Allied troops marched across Germany. On April 4, the 89th Infantry captured the German town of Gotha in south central Germany. Just outside of town was the Ohrdruf concentration camp. It was one of several sub-camps serving the Buchenwald extermination camp, several miles north of Gotha. Ohrdruf was a holding facility for over 11,000 prisoners on the way to the gas chambers and crematoria at Buchenwald. Just before the Americans arrived, the Germans marched all the inmates who could walk to Buchenwald. The rest were killed. When the Americans arrived at Ohrdruf they found thousands of bodies of prisoners who had died from bullet wounds, starvation, abuse, and disease. Bodies were piled throughout the camp. Many of the mounds of dead bodies were still smoldering from failed attempts by the departing Germans to burn them. The stench was horrible. General Eisenhower ordered every American solider in the area not on the front lines to visit Ohrdruf and Buchenwald. Eisenhower said that the atrocities were "beyond the American mind to comprehend." He ordered every German citizen to tour the camp. After doing so, the town mayor and his wife went home and hanged themselves. Eisenhower would later remark that he "never dreamed that such cruelty, bestiality, and savagery could really exist in this world." In the coming months he would order civilian news media and military combat camera units to place their observations in print, pictures, and film. He explained, "I made the visit deliberately, in order to be in a position to give first-hand evidence of these things, if ever, in the future, there develops a tendency to charge these allegations merely to 'propaganda.'[44]" That day has come. There are an increasing number of people around the world who deny the existence of the Holocaust. Most notable is Iran's vocal Islamist leader Mahmoud Ahmadinejad. He has said, "They have created a myth today that they call the massacre of Jews and they consider it a principle above God, religions and the prophets"[45].

Fast forward 56 years later to a bright, cloudless September morning on the East coast of America. Terrorists hijacked four planes and successfully destroyed New York's World Trade Center and parts of the Pentagon in Washington D.C. It is widely believed that the fourth plane was destined to hit the United States Capitol in Washington, before those on board overtook the hijackers. That plane crashed into a field near Shanksville, PA. September 11, 2001 is a day that will go down in infamy. Almost 3000 persons lost their lives that day. Most of the events were recorded on video as they took place. Yet, even with clear evidence, there are a number of people around the world who deny these events were acts of terrorism. They believe 9/11 was a massive conspiracy, perpetuated by the government in order to have an excuse to exert its power over the people. One theory goes like this, "The Twin Towers collapsed because demolition charges were planted inside them, not because of fire and structural damage resulting from American Flight 11 and United Flight 175 plowing into them. The buildings had been designed to withstand great stress and the fires were not hot enough to melt steel. And, if the buildings had collapsed, they would have fallen at an angle—not pancaked straight down, as only buildings destroyed by controlled demolition do."[46] Theories like this ignore the massive amount of time and preparation that would be necessary to plant the number of explosives necessary to take the towers down. It is just a simple rejection of the realness of 9/11.

The denial of the proven reality in these acts of evil is a direct result of darkness, which constantly works to get us to gloss over its horrible effects. Darkness would have us to smooth things over and shift the blame somewhere else. If the Lord tarries and allows time to go on, those who wish to rewrite history will only grow. We must never fall for incursions of darkness, no matter how strong the pressure.

In the darkest moments the world has ever known, Jesus was crucified on a cross outside Jerusalem. All the events of that Thursday and Friday were nothing less than the best efforts of darkness to thwart the marvelous plan of God. How did darkness work at Calvary? How does darkness work to separate us from the gravity of these events? **Do we truly understand how dark the events of Calvary** *really* **were?**

Darkness at work: The last 36 hours of Jesus' life

When Jesus came into the world, Satan's power was turned against Him. From the moment He arrived, Satan continually worked to bring about His destruction. In every possible way he sought to prevent Jesus from developing a perfect childhood, a faultless manhood, a holy ministry, and an unblemished sacrifice. Ultimately he did not succeed. He could not lead Jesus into sin. He could not drive Him from fulfilling God's plan of redemption for mankind. Through Jesus' resurrection, Satan was crushed and dealt a mortal blow, Hebrews 2.14-15.

While we know the outcome, we must not underestimate the work of Satan during the last 36 hours of Jesus' life. This was Satan's last, desperate chance to thwart God's plan. Each second must have felt like a year for Jesus as he weathered the ultimate storm of temptation. In every way possible, Satan and his forces of darkness exerted an intense and focused assault on Jesus, mercilessly oppressing Him. Yet, as Satan pressed, Jesus resisted, clinging to the hand of His father.

The story of Jesus' last hours is contained in Matthew 26.15-27.56; Mark 14.12-15.41; Luke 22.7-23.49; and John 13.1-19.37. As we read these chapters it is important to see how darkness worked.

When we first read of Judas' decision to betray Jesus, Luke tells us that "Satan entered into Judas," who then "went away and conferred with the chief priests and officers how he might betray him to them." Luke 22.3-4. John's gospel also tells us of Satan's activity concerning Judas during this period, John 13.2, 27. Satan knew exactly how to "get to" Judas. His greedy heart is a well known fact by readers of John's gospel, 6.71; 12.4-6. The lure of easy money and the draw of building favor with the Jewish religious leaders was the perfect entry point for darkness. John 11.57 says that the Pharisees had given orders that "if anyone knew where He was, he should let them know." Judas could have easily envisioned monetary reward and a place of recognition by these "powerful" people. Darkness told him that the most important thing was himself. Taking this into consideration, it should be easy to understand why Judas didn't even resist. He allowed Satan to walk right into his heart. As you reread the gospel accounts of Judas' betrayal—he could have stopped at *any* moment. He did not have to go through with it. Darkness hardened his heart.

The conversation recorded in John 13.21-27 is especially interesting. Jesus said one of the 12 would betray him. John, sitting right next to Jesus, leaned back and quietly asked who it was. Jesus said, "It is he to whom I will give this morsel of bread when I have dipped it." 13.26. Then He gave the morsel to Judas and the record says Satan entered his heart. Judas who never made an attempt to resist Satan had hardened himself to the point where there was no turning back. He immediately went out from their presence, 13.30. The depth of this betrayal is absolutely astonishing. Thinking again of the private conversation going on between Jesus and John about the one who would betray Him, why not just tell John directly that it was Judas? Jesus wanted to impress on John the **enormity** of the situation. "Judas was ready to betray the One out of whose very hand he had been fed!" [47] Consider the emotional toll this event must have had upon Jesus. The depth of His suffering would fall to unimaginable levels. Think of the humiliation of being turned in by one of your own for monetary gain. Think of how Satan would have enjoyed twisting the metaphorical knife he had just used to stab Jesus through with the actions of one of those closest to Him.

John 13.30b should not go unnoticed. The record simply says, "and it was night." The fact that many of these events happened in the darkness of night is fitting. What a *dark* night it must have been! Jesus Himself said that men love to do their unrighteous deeds in the dark, John 3.18-20. Make no mistake, Satan was in overdrive that night—using every moment he had to derail Jesus from the mission. The activity of Satan did not stop with Judas. Once Jesus and the disciples leave the house where they had gathered for the Passover meal, they head to the garden of Gethsemane. While there, don't think Satan sat idly by. The level of temptation during these moments must have been agonizing. As Jesus struggled, desperately wanting another way to go through crucifixion, Satan would have worked to reinforce those emotions. Hear Satan tell Jesus that *they just aren't worth this*. Think of how Satan must have worked to magnify the thought of the torture Jesus was about to experience. And yet, three times Jesus resists in the only way He could—through prayer. The emotional toll is almost unbearable, so much so that an angel from heaven appeared, "strengthening Him." Luke 22.43.

After returning from the last time of prayer, Jesus walks back to find his disciples sleeping. As He questioned them, Judas led a band of soldiers to arrest Him. He knew right where to go. Judas knew Jesus would be there praying. He had been there with Jesus before. John describes the soldiers and officers of the chief priests coming with "lanterns, torches, and weapons." John 18.3. They approach Jesus as if He were a criminal! This is the ultimate insult! "Have you come out as against a robber, with swords and clubs to capture me." Matthew 26.55. Jesus saw all of this as an enclosing shroud of darkness: "But this is your hour, and the **power of darkness.**" Luke 22.53. Judas approaches and kisses him! "Judas, the treasurer, the man in whom the others had put their trust, he was now standing with the powers of the prince of darkness." [48]

Dragging Jesus off, shackled by chains, they bring Him before the Jewish Sanhedrin. This body consisted of seventy one members. They had legislative, executive, and judicial power.

There was no appeal available for its decisions. Its authority was supreme in all matters—civil, criminal, political, social, and religious. Darkness was most assuredly at work inside the hearts of these men that night. *Every* aspect of this trial violated their law. Jesus was arrested because of a bribe. Jewish law prohibited any part of legal proceedings by night. [49] Their law also forbade court proceedings to be held on the "eve of the Sabbath, or that of any fesitval." [50] Jesus was asked to incriminate Himself. The entire trial took place over the span of a few hours. In capital cases, Jewish law did not permit the sentence to be pronounced until the day after the accused had been convicted. [51] There was no intention to give Jesus a fair trial. Think of the humilation of being tried before self-seeking and hypocritical men like Annas and Caiaphas. While they worked their evil plan they had to maintain their "purity" in front of the people, John 18.28. This is darkness at work!

Peter's denial of Jesus must have certainly added to the sorrow of the moment. As Jesus entered into the house of the high priest, Peter, who within the previous hour, had sought to boldly strike out at the enemies of Jesus with a sword, shriveled into a shell of his former self. Driven to the point of cursing and swearing, Peter denies his association with Christ a third time. The rooster immediately crowed and "the Lord turned and looked at Peter." Luke 22.61. Who and what caused Peter's courage to evaporate? Who and what is piercing Jesus through with the emotional toll of being rejected by one of his closest companions? We know the answer. Darkness.

Now Pilate enters the scene. As always, darkness exploited the weaknesses of the Roman governor. Throughout the entire process, Pilate's sole focus is on himself. Should he please his wife? The Jews? What would the Emperor think? How would his decision impact his career? There was no concern for anyone else. There was absolutely no consideration for the innocent life that he was going to terminate on a cross. After seeing he could go no further in convincing the Jews to release Jesus, he took water and washed his hands saying, "I am innocent of this man's blood, see to it yourselves." Matthew 27.24b. Darkness influenced him to believe the lie he told himself. It said he had done nothing with Jesus—when he was the only man in the city who could have passed the death sentence. He wasn't responsible. *Someone else was.* Any decision he made was the result of his *being pushed into it.* Pilate attempted to be "neutral" in this situation. But when it comes to Jesus, neutrality is impossible. Due to his own personal weaknesses, Pilate succumbed to intimidation and allowed darkness to do its work.

I believe there is an important reason why we see Pilate's continual declaration of Jesus' innocence. It was meant to communicate that Jesus was not condemned to die because of his own transgressions. It was for the transgressions of the world that He died. "He committed no sin, neither was deceit found in his mouth. When he was reviled, he did not revile in return; when he suffered, he did not threaten, but continued entrusting himself to him who judges justly. He himself bore our sins in his body on the tree, that we might die to sin and live to righteousness. By his wounds you have been healed." 1 Peter 2.22-24. Put more specifically, it was for **our** sins that He died. **Never** forget that.

Darkness also manifested itself that ugly day through a most unlikely character—Barabbas. A notorious robber and murderer, Barabbas was more than deserving of being on a cross that Friday afternoon, Mark 15.7. A greater contrast could not have existed between the two men. Pilate *thought* he had the perfect out. Offer up one for execution and release the other. He figured the people would overwhelmingly choose Barabbas for crucifixion. It didn't happen. His plan failed. What made the crowd choose Barabbas over Jesus? Imagine the utter humiliation and repulsiveness of this moment. Here is Jesus standing next to the vile and insolent Barabbas. Jesus, who minutes earlier had just been declared to be without fault by Pilate, 18.38, is now offered up as a choice in a gruesome contest where the "prize" is a cross. Darkness won. Pilate handed Jesus over to be crucified. Imagine how darkness continued to work on Jesus as He struggled under the weight of His cross, carrying it through the streets of Jerusalem and finally up to Golgotha. All the way to the bitter end, darkness was actively pursuing Jesus.

Then comes the crucifixion itself. As Jesus hangs there, darkness "fell over the whole land.", Luke 23.44. This literal darkness could be interpreted to symbolize the blackness and heavy weight of sin. "For our sake he made him to be sin who knew no sin, so that in him we might become the righteousness of God." 2 Corinthians 5.21. The agony of these moments cannot be over-emphasized. Now in the midst of darkness, Jesus feels completely alone—separated from His father. "My God, my God, why have You forsaken Me." Matthew 27.46. This is a quote from Psalm 22 where the Psalmist asks, "Why are you so far from saving me, from the words of my groaning? O my God, I cry by day, but you do not answer, and by night, but I find no rest., Psalm 22.1b-2.

Then He died. For the next 36 hours, all appeared lost. Satan probably thought he was the ruler of the world. Had evil *really* triumphed?

We understand Jesus had to die. But why the cross?

Three centuries before Jesus, ancient peoples devised one of the most terrible forms of execution ever known to man. The Romans took crucifixion and perfected it to the point where the condemned individual experienced as much humiliation and agony as possible. A person could expect to die a slow, painful, gruesome, and public death. Some individuals lingered for days before finally succumbing. After death, the victim was often left hanging on the cross as a display to warn others that the authorities were serious about punishing lawbreakers.

Hundreds of years before Jesus, the prophets foretold of His suffering on the cross. In prophetic writings, David said, "I am... scorned by mankind and despised by the people. All who see me mock me; they make mouths at me; they wag their heads. I am poured out like water; and all my bones are out of joint; my strength is dried up and my tongue sticks to my jaws; they have pierced my hands and feet. They stare and gloat over me. They divide my garments among them, and for my clothing they cast lots." Psalm 22.6-7, 14-15, 17-18. Isaiah also said, "He was wounded for our transgressions; he was crushed for our iniquities; upon Him was the chastisement that brought us peace and with His stripes we are healed." Isaiah 53.5.

When Adam and Eve succumbed to temptation, sin entered our world. Those who transgress God's law, commit sin, 1 John 1.4. Sin has a terrible price: **death**, Romans 6.23. All are guilty of sin and it is Jesus who rescued us from this predicament through His sacrifice. By offering Himself for us, Jesus turned away the wrath of God. Paul wrote, "all have sinned and fall short of the glory of God, and are justified by his grace as a gift, through the redemption that is in Christ Jesus, whom God put forward as a propitiation by his blood, to be received by faith. This was to show God's righteousness, because in his divine forbearance he had passed over former sins. It was to show his righteousness at the present time, so that he might be just and the justifier of the one who has faith in Jesus.", Romans 3.23-26.

From this passage, we clearly see that Jesus had to die. A person can die many different ways. Why crucifixion? Why the cross? Sin is hideous. Sin is repulsive. Sin is reprehensible. Sin is an affront to the justice and righteousness of God. It is polluted, miserable, and filthy. It is degrading and shameful. It binds a person into captivity. It renders a person hopeless. God used the cross as a visible symbol to demonstrate the vileness of sin and to prove the lengths He was willing to go to save us from sin. **Jesus became a curse for us.** Jewish law said that a hanged man is cursed by God, Deuteronomy 21.23. He stood in our place. Jesus was not guilty of our sin, but bore the punishment for **our** transgressions. He committed no sin, neither was deceit found in His mouth. "He Himself bore our sins in His body on the tree, that we might die to sin and live to righteousness. By His wounds you have been healed." 1 Peter 2.22, 24. Jesus died so that all humankind can be saved, Galatians 3.13-14. Jesus released us from the bondage and chains of sin. His death brings freedom and hope. "In my Father's house are many rooms. If it were not so, would I have told you that I go to prepare a place for you? And if I go and prepare a place for you, I will come again and will take you to myself, that where I am you may be also." John 14.2-3.

Jesus died to free us from sin and give us hope. In speaking of Him, John the Baptist described Jesus as "the Lamb of God, who takes away the sin of the world." John 1.29.

We must make the connection.

It is very hard to reread the accounts of the Passion of the Christ and not be emotionally stirred. When we consider the intense sorrow, pain of betrayal, blood spilled, and the torturous six hours Jesus spent nailed on the side of a tree, our hearts break. When we picture the smug smiles on the faces of the Pharisees and Sadducees and the mocking of the Roman soldiers it is difficult not to feel a twinge of righteous anger. We might marvel at those in the crowd that day. How could *anyone* have stood there gawking at such a grotesque scene? We become frustrated at the impotence of the Roman governor who allowed himself to be intimidated by hypocritical and calloused religious leaders. We shake our heads at the shortsightedness and ignorant foolishness of Judas, who allowed his insatiable desire for money, prestige, and power to move him to betray Jesus for 30 pieces of silver. We shudder as we think of what could have been, had Judas only repented like Peter. The darkness of *that* day was *real* in every *aspect*.

Darkness has an uncanny ability to convince us that it is not as bad as it *really* is. We must ask, *have we allowed this to happen with the cross?* Now that time has separated us from that day by a span of around 2000 years, **is it real to us?** Have we made the connection that it was our sin that put Jesus on the cross? Darkness deludes us into thinking that we are not so bad. Jesus died for all the *really bad* people in the world. The problem is, **we are that really bad person.**

This matter is highly **personal.** "He has borne *our* griefs and carried *our* sorrows; yet *we* esteemed Him stricken, smitten by God, and afflicted. But He was pierced for *our* transgressions;

88

He was crushed for *our* iniquities." Isaiah 53.4-5. Paul said that "He was delivered up for our trespasses." Romans 4.25. Peter said, "He Himself bore *our* sins in His body on the tree." 1 Peter 2.24. Paul includes himself and **every person** in the list of **ungodly enemies** who were aligned against God when He decided to send Jesus to die in our place, Romans 5.6-10. If we were the only person on earth, rebellious, dirty and stained with sin, God would have enacted His great scheme for **our** redemption. God's love and compassion for us is personal—just as our defiant and insubordinate actions were once personally against Him.

Darkness seeks to separate or disconnect us from this fact. If it can get us to delete the personal connection with Jesus' rescue from sin, it has the upper hand. Darkness moves to keep us away from the *brokenness* that is necessary to receive the gospel as God intends. We must come to God conscious of the reality that exists, realizing our vile condition before Him, and confessing our need for His cleansing power. If it can convince us that we are somehow disconnected from the awfulness at Calvary it will send our spiritual life into continual dysfunction. Until we make it personal, our spiritual lives will never prosper as they should.

For Thought and Reflection:

- In betraying Jesus, what was so attractive to Judas?

- Describe the shame and humiliation that comes packaged inside the act of betrayal.

- What would Satan's method of attack have been as Jesus entered the garden of Gethsemane?

- What were some of the illegalities associated with the trial of Jesus?

- Who and what caused Peter's courage to evaporate? What emotional toll would this have had on Jesus?

- Did Pilate succeed in his plan to be "neutral" with Jesus? How? What lessons are there for us in this?

- How did darkness work through Barabbas?

- What did the literal darkness that fell over the land while Jesus was on the cross symbolize?

- Name two reasons why God used the cross as Jesus' instrument of death?

- Today, what does darkness attempt to tell us about the cross?

- Why is *brokenness* so important as we approach our relationship with God?

- How can darkness hamper our relationship with God through the lack of a personal connection with the events of Calvary?

When You No Longer Fear Darkness

In December 2009, Salt Lake City resident Josh Powell took his two boys, ages 3 and 5 out for a midnight camping trip in the central Utah desert. That same night their mother, Susan, disappeared. She has never been seen since. Authorities searched for weeks, but were unsuccessful. In the months afterward, Powell's father, Steve, claimed to have had a sexual relationship with Susan. During the summer of 2010, one of the boys drew a picture of a van with three people inside. He told his caregivers that it was a picture of his family going camping. When asked where his mother was, the boy answered, "Mommy's in the trunk. [52]" While Josh Powell had become a "person of interest" in his wife's death, he was never charged with her murder. To date, a body has never been found, although authorities are certain she is no longer alive.

But this story does not end with the tragedy of cold blooded murder. Within one month of Susan Powell's disappearance, her husband moved to the Seattle suburb of Puyallup. Over the last two years Powell faced increasing scrutiny about the disappearance of his wife and an unending custody battle with his in-laws over who would keep his boys.

Powell painted himself as a victim. He often claimed he was tortured and ridiculed without reason concerning the disappearance of his wife. He never admitted to killing her. He told a judge, "A lesser person would fall under the intense scrutiny I am facing, but apparently my inherent resilience as a person makes it increasingly difficult for them to pursue their agendas. I am standing tall for my sons, but it deeply hurts to face such ridicule and abuse. I know my own heart is free of any guilt regardless of what people claim." [53] But, any confidence Powell exhibited quickly evaporated when the court ruled against him in the custody case on February 2, 2012, ordering his children to stay with Susan Powell's parents.

On Sunday, February 5, 2012, Powell was scheduled to have a routine supervised visit with his sons, now ages 5 and 7. When the boys got out of the car, they ran ahead of the social worker and went inside Powell's home. Powell locked the door and hacked them in the neck and head with a hatchet. He then lit the house on fire. All 3 died of smoke inhalation. The fire was not an accident. Just minutes before the boys arrived, he sent out a number of emails to different people saying, "I'm sorry. Goodbye." To others, he sent out instructions on where to find his money and shut off his utilities. In another email he is said to have written that he could not live without his boys.

Powell's murder-suicide is pure evil. It challenges our mind to comprehend it. But it also reveals to us the hardening effects of sin. When darkness moves us to willingly trespass against God, it becomes increasingly easy to make other decisions that move us farther into its shadows. This story demonstrates the hopelessness that is created when God is nowhere in the picture. And finally, it should instill within us a fear of what could happen if we choose to reject God and invite darkness back into our life. Darkness will lead one to places that will change them into a person they cannot recognize.

What happens when we no longer fear darkness?

The Hardening Aspects of Sin

"Take care, brothers, lest there be in any of you an evil, unbelieving heart, leading you to fall away from the living God." Hebrews 3.12. These words come at the end of a section where the Hebrew writer points his Jewish audience back to their forefathers whose rebellion caused them to perish in the wilderness. At first, we may wonder how anyone who had personally witnessed the plagues in Egypt, the parting of the Red Sea, and the shaking mountain at Sinai would ever harden their hearts in unbelief. What the writer of Hebrews is referring to is the end result of a progression of sin that started in the hours after escaping from Egypt. One faithless event will lead to another. As the occasions of rejecting God continued, Israel found it increasingly easy to consciously disregard God and His blessings.

While we may shake our heads in disbelief at the stubborn rebellion of Israel, we can very easily follow the same path to destruction. Today, how many witness the blessings and power of God clearly at work and remain unmoved? How many see the glory and expanse of God's creation and fail to give Him credit? How many observe the power of redemption offered through the cross and are ambivalent? How many choose not to believe at all? How many have been raised in godly homes, know and understand the truth of the gospel, and after entering adulthood walk away?

We know the answer to these questions. We should soberly reflect on the reasons why. Throughout our study we have examined the delusional power of darkness. Sin deceives. It calls darkness light. It says something bitter is sweet. It labels bondage as liberty. It identifies all that is wrong as right. As it lurks, it whispers that there will be little or no consequences for its indulgences. Sin drags us into a state of unbelief. It's a slow progression. It rarely happens overnight. At the beginning of this process, it may be very hard to imagine the end result. **Never, *never* say you are not vulnerable.** If you harden your heart into a state of unbelief, you will be locked out of God's blessings forever. There will be nothing left to move you back to the point of belief.

Israel constantly "put God to the test" and continually saw God's marvelous works, Hebrews 3.9. Yet they boldly engaged in faithless rebellion. Consider the events of Numbers 13-14. God promised that the land of Canaan was their gift from Him. When God commanded them to send in the twelve spies, His desire was to prove *once and for all* that He is a God that is true to His word. Canaan was as God described. It flowed with *milk and honey* and plentifully yielded fruit, 13.27. But, the *horizontal* faith of ten *unbelieving* spies prevailed. The people rebelled. "All the congregation raised a loud cry, and the people wept that night. And all the people of Israel grumbled against Moses and Aaron. The whole congregation said to them, "Would that we had died in the land of Egypt! Or would that we had died in this wilderness! Why is the LORD bringing us into this land, to fall by the sword? Our wives and our little ones will become prey. Would it not be better for us to go back to Egypt?" And they said to one another, "Let us choose a leader and go back to Egypt." Numbers 14.1-4. When Joshua and Caleb responded with a passionate call to launch forward in faith, the people took up stones to stone them, 14.10. As they did, the glory of God descended into the tent of meeting. God voiced His displeasure. "But truly, as I live, and as all the earth shall be filled with the glory of the LORD, none of the men who have seen my glory and my signs that I did in Egypt and in the wilderness, and yet have put me to the test these *ten* times and have not obeyed my voice."14.21-22. [54] There was nothing left. If sending spies into the land to verify all the promises of God wouldn't convince them that God would deliver on His promises, nothing would. The people had closed their hearts and God made the decision to refuse them entrance into Canaan.

Israel never opened their heart to God. Why? Darkness. Satan and his forces live to thwart God's plans at every turn. Darkness convinced Israel to see no further than their physical sight allowed. Darkness lied, telling them that they had it better as slaves in Egypt than God's rescued and delivered *children* in the wilderness. As they quarreled, complained and continued to reject God, their hearts became seared.

It has been said *the same sun that melts wax hardens clay.* There is a *searing power* embedded inside sin that works on the surface of our heart. Sin wounds. Afterward, scar tissue builds over the surface, numbing all feeling of remorse and guilt. Once our hearts become completely numb, there is no end to the downward progression. "A wicked man puts on a bold face, but the upright gives thought to his ways." Proverbs 21.29.

What kind of heart do we possess? Will we fully surrender to God? Today, many refuse. Why? For some it is the lure of the pleasures of the flesh and material possessions. For others it is self reliance and the glory of their own abilities and plans. Even still, there are those who *intellectually* accept the gospel and go no farther. To them the gospel may have been presented as little more than adherence to a five step plan and continued *behavior modification.* It is not enough just to "like" the gospel. Many hear it. Many know it. What they adhere to is agreeable to them and it fits well inside their social structure. But, they never fully commit to Jesus *from the heart.* Then the struggles come and Satan wins a few battles. Rationalization sets in. As time progresses, it becomes easier and easier to just walk away.

Hebrews 3.13 serves as a stern warning concerning a deadly process that leads to dulled spiritual perception. "But exhort one another every day, as long as it is called "today," that none of you may be hardened by the deceitfulness of sin." In the original language, hardening described the procession that makes a spiritual heart "dry or hard."[55] Our hearts can become lifeless. Dead to what? "The living God." 3.12. This is not about rejecting *religion.* It is referring to walking away from the *living God.* Is there anything more tragic than willfully and smugly standing *apart* from God? When we choose *anything* but God, we choose **death.**

What It Means to be in Darkness

"It is a fearful thing to fall into the hands of the living God." Hebrews 10.31. These could be nominated as the fourteen scariest words in all of Scripture. For those who harden their heart and reject God with constant rebellion, a day of reckoning awaits. Judgment day will not be a day filled with glee. Every person will humbly stand before God. "For we must all appear before the judgment seat of Christ, so that each one may receive what is due for what he has done in the body, whether good or evil." 2 Corinthians 5.10. Those who stand before Him condemned will be cast into "outer darkness; in that place there will be weeping and gnashing of teeth." Matthew 25.30.

Next we will learn more about the eternal destiny of darkness. But what of the spiritual darkness a person experiences when he or she determines to step out of the light during this life, between now and the judgment?

Those who walk away are separated from God. When we continue to engage *in the practice of sin,* we are dwelling in darkness. "No one who abides in him keeps on sinning; no one who keeps on sinning has either seen him or known him. Whoever makes a practice of sinning is of the devil, for the devil has been sinning from the beginning." 1 John 3.6, 8. With the absence of God, a person is forced to dwell in this life without the illuminating ways of God. Think of the danger this presents.

A few years ago, I had an opportunity to explore a wild cave. *Bear Trap Cave* got its name from the rancher who explored it during the 1940s. After crawling inside the small entrance and continuing about 30 feet, he found himself on a ledge above a good-sized room. He was about 10 feet above the floor. After bringing in a ladder to lower himself into the room, he found the remains of a bear which must have fallen inside many years before and perished. On the cold, snowy October day my friends and I explored the cave, we were excited to find no wild animals were using the cave as a den. Once we climbed down into the room that had served as the infamous *bear trap*, we continued deeper into the cavern. As we kept going down, we observed the path we were on was actually a ledge overlooking another room. At one point it became extremely narrow and was nothing more than a slippery slope into the blackness on our left. It was only later that we realized we were moving above a giant room whose floor was 30 feet below. Had our lights become inoperable, we would have been in a great deal of trouble. That far in, there was no natural light seeping into the cave. A fall could have resulted in severe injuries, or worse.

In such conditions, it is easy to see the danger of walking in total darkness. Isn't it the same when we try to proceed without spiritual illumination? **We will fall, and fall again, and again.** Every time we sin, we are bruised and battered. The wounds of sin pierce us through. As we descend into this black hole, the sins we commit can create a landslide of consequences that will almost crush us. Some are so trapped in the effects of their sin that an exit seems hopeless. And once Satan convinces a person that he or she is in a hopeless situation, it's over. He's won.

No wonder we see such misery in our world. Living without God and the true *light* His word provides, danger lurks at every turn. Think of those who enter into darkness and wind up wounded and broken. Crushed by the weight of their own sin, they may feel there is no way out of the hole they've walked into. A few years ago God gave the local church family I worked with a wonderful opportunity to help a person who had been stumbling around in the world for a long period of time. Her life was a tangled mess. Divorced for many years, from an unfaithful husband, she had moved to the next state south to begin a new life. She soon fell in love with a man who had walked out of his marriage a few years before. They moved in with each other and wound up having a child together. Not long after revealing her pregnancy, the man decided to move on to another "friend" he met. Now in middle age, alone, with a baby, and very little money to live on she had no where to turn. When she came to us, the emotional baggage was incredible. The feelings of being twice betrayed, worry over the custody of her daughter, and other family issues were intense. She was broken. She desperately wanted out. Thankfully, God provided a way out through His forgiveness. But, the years of dwelling in darkness had taken their toll. Her sinful life had produced extreme consequences that both she and her baby would have to endure for many years to come.

Do we forget those who are all around us, needing to be rescued? Do we see them for the condition they are *really* in? Do we sense the *danger* they face? How many people do you interact with each day that are dwelling in darkness, with the light of God notably absent from their lives? What will we do to help? Who is someone you can rescue?

We Must Fear Being Without God

Evil is real. Sin is vicious. Satan joyfully exploits our every weakness and assaults our every strength. The forces of darkness always lurk. Without God to equip and defend us, defeat would be guaranteed. We stand in *"His strength* and in the power of His might." Ephesians 6.10. For the son or daughter of God, it is hard to imagine facing this world without the lamp of God's word shedding light onto our path.

Without God, we are completely out in the open and vulnerable to every device of darkness. There is a reason why the Holy Spirit repeatedly refers to God as our Shepherd. The metaphor would have most certainly resonated with the agrarian culture of biblical Israel. When we choose darkness, we willingly exit the protection He provides. When they left the fold, sheep were in danger of lion and bear attacks, starvation, and endless wandering. David's job as a shepherd gives us some insight into the dangers that were associated with this profession, 1 Samuel 17.34-36.

When we continually choose to walk away from God, we place ourselves in the throws of danger. "Your adversary the devil prowls around like a roaring lion, seeking someone to devour." 1 Peter 5.8. While fear is not the only motivator, it is certainly *a* motivator that keeps us inside the fold of God. We need to fear Satan, because he is real and the destruction he wants to lead us toward is equally real. The pain he inflicts on those in his grasp is something we should steer away from at all costs. We need to possess a healthy fear of what it means to be without God.

In Psalm 56, we see David's emotional state as he fled from Saul. David felt like he had nowhere to go and went to Gath which was located deep inside the territory of the Philistines, 1 Samuel 21.10-15. At the time, this decision must have made sense. But by going into the darkness of Philistia, David felt alone, vulnerable, and afraid. "Be gracious to me, O God, for man tramples on me; all day long an attacker oppresses me; my enemies trample on me all day long, for many attack me proudly. All day long they injure my cause; all their thoughts are against me for evil. They stir up strife, they lurk; they watch my steps, as they have waited for my life." Psalm 56.1-2, 5-6. His great fear explains his actions in 1 Samuel 21.13.

As we continue reading Psalm 56, what sustained David? God. "For their crime will they escape? In wrath cast down the peoples, O God! Then my enemies will turn back in the day when I call. This I know, that God is for me. In God I trust; I shall not be afraid. What can man do to me? I must perform my vows to you, O God; I will render thank offerings to you. For you have delivered my soul from death, yes, my feet from falling, that I may walk before God in the light of life." Psalm 56.7, 9, 11-13.

Today, as long as we walk in the light, we have the assurance of God's continual presence and protection. "We know that everyone who has been born of God does not keep on sinning, but he who was born of God protects him, and the evil one does not touch him. We know that we are from God, and the whole world lies in the power of the evil one. And we know that the Son of God has come and has given us understanding, so that we may know him who is true; and we are in him who is true, in his Son Jesus Christ. He is the true God and eternal life." 1 John 5.18-20.

Conclusion

In this life, we may never know who murdered Susan Powell. But we can clearly see the effects of darkness and how it destroyed the lives of two parents and ultimately the two innocent children that marriage produced. Satan wants to harden your heart and lead you down the path of destruction. Will you let him?

For Thought and Reflection

- Describe the delusional power of darkness.

- Describe the *searing power* of sin.

- What are some factors we face today that could lead to the hardening of our heart?

- What happens when we engage *in the practice* of sin?

- What is the danger of living in spiritual darkness?

- What keeps us from seeing the danger that those in the world face? What will happen when we truly realize their condition?

- What dangers lurk for those who choose to wander outside the fold?

- Describe David's emotional state as he entered Gath. Why would he have felt this way?

- Of what are we assured as we *walk in the light?*

Eternal Destiny and Darkness

Introduction:

At Harvard Divinity School, theologian Gordon Kaufman researched over four centuries of the decline in the concepts of heaven and hell. "What is left," he said, "is intellectually empty baggage. It seems to me we've gone through irreversible changes. I don't think there can be any future in heaven and hell." [56] Kaufman's statement is amazing. God's word clearly and decisively teaches that one place or the other will be our destiny once this life is over!

Heaven or hell awaits. Pause for a moment and think about the last time you have heard preaching on or studied a Bible class lesson about the ultimate destiny of the unbeliever. Do you remember? Has it been a long time? We just don't talk about *outer darkness* very much anymore. Maybe it is because it is uncomfortable. We are afraid that *negative* messages turn off seekers. Long acceptable in the most liberal of churches, there is now a growing number of individuals in conservative churches that believe the biblical concept of eternal punishment is outdated and not suitable for today's audiences. Whatever the reason, our general avoidance of this topic is leading to consequences that are starting to take their toll. Research finds:

- One survey of evangelical seminary students revealed that almost half (46%) felt that preaching about hell to unbelievers is in "poor taste." [57]

- 64% of Americans expect to go to heaven when they die, but less than 1% think they might go to hell. [58]

- Half of Americans (50%) believe that all people are eventually saved or accepted by God no matter what they do, while 40% disagreed. [59]

What if things progress to where a large majority of Americans no longer believe in hell? Will the facts change? "If every person on earth voted that there is no hell, it would not lower its temperature one degree. If there is a hell, then there is one, and what men and women believe does not change it. Missionaries in some hot climates have been unable to convince natives that ice exists. They just can't believe that water can become so hard that a man could walk on it. Does this change the fact that ice exists?" [60] It matters very little what we *think* about hell. It is a very real place. Heaven or hell will be our eternal destiny once this life is completed. Paul wrote, "He will render to each one according to his works: to those who by patience in well-doing seek for glory and honor and immortality, he will give eternal life; but for those who are self-seeking and do not obey the truth, but obey unrighteousness, there will be wrath and fury. There will be tribulation and distress for every human being who does evil, the Jew first and also the Greek, but glory and honor and peace for everyone who does good, the Jew first and also the Greek." Romans 2.6-10.

Actions have consequences. There will be a day of reckoning for every unrepentant sinner. The choices we make in our attitude and behaviors will determine our eternal destiny. Jesus sternly warned, "For the Son of Man is going to come with his angels in the glory of his Father, and then he will repay each person according to what he has done." Matthew 16.27. He also said, "Enter by the narrow gate. For the gate is wide and the way is easy that leads to destruction, and those who enter by it are many. For the gate is narrow and the way is hard that leads to life, and those who find it are few." Matthew 7.13-14. Which road are you on?

Today's Cultural Attitude Toward Hell is the Work of Darkness.

There is a great spiritual war going on. It takes place every day inside the battlefield of our mind. Darkness constantly works to diminish the harshness of its reality. This has always been the case—in the spiritual realm and the physical. In the years leading up to World War II, the Nazi party worked tirelessly to instill pride in Germany, restore a shattered economy, and build good will with public works projects. The propaganda campaign was cleverly designed to shroud the evil going on behind the scenes. Hitler and his comrades were so successful that some Germans refused to see the reality of the Nazi darkness until being forced by General Eisenhower to walk through the concentration camps and see the carnage for themselves.

It is no different in the spiritual realm. Satan constantly distracts us with the cares of this world and whispers that death happens to everyone else but us. Think of how effective the forces of darkness have been inside our own culture over the last sixty years. Millions fall prey to the lie every day. For some, the realization of eternity comes only after stepping into it after an untimely death. Once we cross over, there is no turning back. There are no second chances. We see this with the rich man mentioned in Luke 16:19-31. In torment in hades (the waiting place of the dead until judgment), the man was very conscious and in torment. His thoughts drifted to his family who were still alive. He in no way wanted them to experience what he did. For him, there was only *eternity* ahead, forever separated from God.

Darkness constantly tells us not to think about or talk about death. While certainly not pleasant to dwell upon, its coming is a fact for every person. Someday, we will all die. "It is appointed for man to die once, and after that comes judgment." Hebrews 9.27. Not only are we all subject to it, it can touch us at any time. It might come at old age. It could come at mid-life or after a long illness. It could come in the midst of our sleep, a car wreck, walking down the street, or while on vacation. Wealth and power can't stop it. Moral goodness can't hold it back. It could come during the teen years or in the midst of childhood. But it will come. "It is the same for all, since the same event happens to the righteous and the wicked, to the good and the evil, to the clean and the unclean, to him who sacrifices and him who does not sacrifice. As the good one is, so is the sinner, and he who swears is as he who shuns an oath. For the living know that they will die." Ecclesiastes 9.2, 5a. If darkness can succeed in getting us to ignore the fact of our death, the greater its opportunity to lead us away from heaven. **We must spend this life preparing for our death.** Solomon said, "The end of the matter; all has been heard. Fear God and keep his commandments, for this is the whole duty of man. For God will bring every deed into judgment, with every secret thing, whether good or evil." Ecclesiastes 12.13-14.

Darkness says that it is OK to *temporarily* put off the spiritual in exchange for a few years of fun. How many of our young people get trapped in the thinking that says they can deal with salvation some point later in time? Satan says go out and *get the best of what life has to offer, you deserve it.* Darkness promises that there will be plenty of time for living for God later. For some, *later* never comes. Pick up today's obituary section in your local paper. It is very likely that you can easily find a listing of someone who has recently died, *unexpectedly*, long before they ever imagined they would. Accidents happen. Evil abounds. Disease strikes. In a moment it can all change and the opportunity is *eternally* lost. Once a person makes a decision to put God off, it becomes easier at later points in the progression of life. Young married couples and college kids immerse themselves in a career and soon find their spiritual commitment derailed. *I'll come back to the Lord when we have children. I'm just too busy trying to get ahead right now.* Then mid-life comes, then old age, and darkness still whispers, *wait.* Every day of life moves us closer to a great precipice. Are you ready to cross over? There is a great day coming! Don't let darkness convince you that your life is anything but uncertain. Don't let it dull your senses to the stinging reality of death.

Darkness has been particularly effective in lulling American Christians to sleep with an entertainment driven culture. Professional sports, college sports, high school, and youth league sports have become the new religion in America. Our country exalts its entertainment figures into icons and allows them to parade their immoral behavior in movies, music, and on television. Flags are lowered at half staff when celebrities who destroyed their life with illegal drugs die. [61] Millions are infatuated with finding fifteen minutes of fame on reality television. Sports and entertainment rule. It seems as if we live to be distracted from the realities that are all around and certain to come. "When we need to be dreaming, for the glory of Christ, about how to spend our lives alleviating ignorance, sickness, misery, and lostness, we are becoming more and more addicted to amusement." [62] As a nation, Americans seem to be *amusing* themselves all the way to eternal damnation.

Darkness tricks us into watering down passages that warn us about the severity of God's wrath. There is a very real teaching in Romans 11.22: "Note then the kindness and the severity of God: severity toward those who have fallen, but God's kindness to you, provided you continue in his kindness. Otherwise you too will be cut off." Here we learn about the goodness and the severity of God. We need to see both sides of the nature of God. See also Hebrews 10.26-31. Here the Hebrew writer speaks of:

- "Fearful expectation of judgment, and a fury of fire that will consume the adversaries." 10.27.

- "Vengeance is Mine, I will repay." 10.30b.

- "It is a fearful thing to fall into the hands of the living God.", 10.31.

Many inside our culture would rather pretend that these verses do not exist. To them, God is more of a teddy bear than a righteous judge. Many would much rather view Him through the eyes of a soft and tender friend and ignore the fact that He will righteously punish the wicked with His fury and vengeance. We must not focus on one side of God to the exclusion of the other. We must be impressed with the fact that a loving and compassionate Father will still throw a rebellious sinner into hell! While He is love, 1 John 4.8, He will never tolerate unrighteousness, 2 Thessalonians 1.8-9.

Darkness is now working through influential religious leaders who teach their followers that hell is not eternal. In 2011, evangelical leader Rob Bell published the controversial book, *Love Wins*. Bell is not the first to change his belief on the eternalness of outer darkness. The idea of a non-eternal hell has been popular in the more liberal religious circles for the last century and a half. Now, the belief is finding itself more and more within churches of Christ. In early 2012, Ed Fudge will be releasing a movie on how his thoughts of this subject evolved. [63] In 2003, Nevada Publications posthumously released Homer Hailey's book, *God's Judgments and Punishments*, which promotes the annihilationist viewpoint. Over the next few decades, we should expect this doctrine to move more into the mainstream thinking of many New Testament Christians.

Some might be quick to dismiss the argument over *eternal torture in hell* as just another preacher squabble. We might be inclined to think, what does it *really* matter? *I don't want to experience eternal death period, whether it ends with the destruction of my soul or in unending, eternal torment.* This is an important subject. It must not be ignored. The difference between believing in the doctrine of eternal suffering in hell and simply ceasing to exist could not be greater. What punishment is there in annihilation? Think of the countless people who have committed acts of genocide and evil who, rather than suffer through punishment and humiliation, seek their own death as an escape. When Saddam Hussein was captured in 2004, American and Iraqi soldiers constantly guarded him, making it impossible for him to cheat justice by committing suicide. "Every knee will bow," Philippians 2.10, and every person will face God and "give an account of himself to God." Romans 14.12. Those who stand condemned will not be able to escape the wrath of God in the fires of hell. "Then the kings of the earth and the great ones and the generals and the rich and the powerful, and everyone, slave and free, hid themselves in the caves and among the rocks of the mountains, calling to the mountains and rocks, 'Fall on us and hide us from the face of him who is seated on the throne, and from the wrath of the Lamb, for the great day of their wrath has come, and who can stand.'" Revelation 6.15-17.

What the Bible says about *Outer Darkness*.

When we examine the preaching of Jesus, we understand His first emphasis on God's goodness and love. But Jesus was never embarrassed to warn of the reality and awfulness of hell. In eleven different scripture references, Jesus related this reality. In fact, most of what we know about hell and outer darkness comes from Jesus. He taught about it more than all other Biblical authors put together. If our Savior thought the matter was of such vital importance, we owe it to ourselves to come to a better understanding of God's divine justice.

The awfulness of hell cannot be overstated. Jesus and His Apostles described it in this way:

A place of eternal fire, Matthew 25.41, 46. Revelation 20.10 speaks of how the devil and his angels will be tormented forever, day and night. This is not annihilation, but sheer darkness filled with conscious, suffering beings.

A place where an unquenchable fire exists, Matthew 13.42, 50; Mark 9.43-48. If souls will be burned up into a state of unconsciousness, why the need for an unquenchable fire? Perhaps one of the most terrifying passages in the entire Bible is found in Revelation 14.11: "And the smoke of their torment goes up forever and ever, *and they have no rest,* day or night, these worshipers of the beast and its image, and whoever receives the mark of its name." If the smoke of their torment goes up forever and ever, they must be suffering throughout all eternity. A powerful contrast is seen in 14.13: "Blessed are the dead who die in the Lord from now on." "Blessed indeed," says the Spirit, *'that they may rest from their labors,* for their deeds follow them!'" The word rest in 14.11 and 14.13 is significant. Those who die in the Lord have *rest* from their labors. But, the beast worshippers have *no rest* day or night. Nowhere in Scripture do we find a promise of rest for the lost. Those who go to hell will experience continual, unceasing, and conscious torment.

A place of weeping and gnashing of teeth, Matthew 8.12; 13.42, 50; 22.13; 24.51; 25.30; Luke 13.28. These expressions are used to describe the mental anguish of utter sorrow and regret. In several of these passages, hell is presented as *a furnace of fire* that produces "weeping and gnashing of teeth." There is no mention anywhere of instantaneous extinction. Imagine experiencing eternity and constantly living with the consequences of the bad choices made while in this life. Part of the torture associated with outer darkness is the continual remembrance and regret of one's rejection of God.

A place of outer darkness, Matthew 8.12; 22.13; 2 Peter 2.17; Jude 3. By using the term outer *darkness,* Jesus intended to communicate the complete and eternal separation from God. Extraction from this darkness will never happen. Those who wind up there will be in the ultimate hopeless situation. In Matthew 7.21-23; 25.41; and Luke 13.27 the word *depart* is used. Those who spend eternity in hell will continually experience the eternal pain of rejection, loneliness, and void of the blessings of God. There is no more terrifying statement one could hear than the one that Jesus will say to the condemned. "Depart from me, you cursed, into the eternal fire prepared for the devil and his angels." Matthew 25.41. Nothing is more important in this life than living in such a way to avoid such a condemnation. "What will it profit a man if he gains the whole world and forfeits his soul? Or what shall a man give in return for his soul." Matthew 16.26.

Conclusion

Hell was never intended for man. God wishes that all persons be saved. Peter said, "The Lord is not slow to fulfill his promise as some count slowness, but is patient toward you, not wishing that any should perish, but that all should reach repentance." 2 Peter 3.9. While hell was designed for Satan and his angels, all who serve Satan will spend eternity there. All who reject God and live for themselves will be there, 1 Corinthians 6.9-11. All who refuse to obey the gospel will be there, 2 Thessalonians 1.7-9.

The good news is that **no one has to go there.** By the grace of God, through the sacrifice of Jesus on the cross, we can escape the fires of hell and enjoy eternity in heaven. Don't let darkness convince you that there is no future in heaven and hell. One or the other is our future and God wants us to spend eternity with Him!

For Thought and Reflection

- Why do we not like to talk about death or eternal punishment?

- What are some ways Satan may be seeking to distract you from the reality of eternity?

- Why is it so important to spend this life preparing for our death? See Ecclesiastes 12.13-14.

- How can sports and entertainment lull us into spiritual sleep?

- What does Romans 11.22 say about the nature of God?

- Which side of God does popular culture focus on? Why?

- Is the doctrinal disagreement over *eternal punishment* in hell an important issue? Why?

- As you read the biblical description of hell, what scares you most?

- Do the condemned have any promise of receiving *rest* from their punishment? Why or why not?

The Hopelessness of Darkness

Introduction:

On a late fall evening, my flight departed New York's JFK airport and headed south along the East coast on a flight to Colombia. As we took off, passengers on the right side of the plane were treated to an incredible view of the entire Tri-State area. Flying over New York City at night is a treat. The sea of lights goes on forever, and the view of the skyscrapers of Manhattan in the distance is simply impressive. If there ever were a demonstration of our country's material blessings and ingenuity it would be here. As we headed south, the lights of America's eastern seaboard served as a map of where we were. Within an hour and a half, Miami and Ft. Lauderdale were vividly illuminated and then, at last, we headed out over the Gulf of Mexico. Within minutes we looked down on Cuba. Darkness ruled. From my vantage point, only an occasional, isolated light could be seen here and there. It was a far cry from what we had just witnessed only eighty miles north. Another hour and a half later we passed directly over Jamaica. It seemed that the entire island was completely dark—with the exception of Kingston, which on a much smaller scale, rivaled the brightest lights of some of America's largest cities.

It is hard for most Americans to understand what real physical darkness is. We are rarely in it. Even in the most desolate of places there is usually enough light pollution to enable us to see how to get around. But pause for a moment and consider utter darkness with absolutely no light source. You can't see your hand just a few inches from your face. If you have ever experienced this type of darkness, the situation can be quite terrifying. There is nowhere to go without danger. The fear of the unknown and uncertainty in movement can paralyze even the bravest of individuals.

Staying in a condition of utter darkness for a prolonged period of time can be mentally devastating. In 1914, British explorer Ernest Shackleton led a crew of men to Antarctica. Their plan was to walk across the continent from one side to the other crossing the South Pole as they went along. As they traveled south on the ship *Endurance,* their boat got caught up in sea ice and became frozen in place. It was January 15, 1915. Out of radio contact and stranded where there was no hope of rescue, the 28 men in Shackleton's expedition camped on pack ice a mile and a half away from the ship. By mid May, the light of day had disappeared. For around 60 days each winter, all of Antarctica is shrouded in total darkness. It is hard for us to imagine how it would feel to endure the extreme level of darkness, cold, and weather an Antarctic winter brings. Each day proved to be a test of the human will to survive. After 281 days, the ship was broken up by the ice and sank on November 21, 1915. On December 20, Shackleton decided it was time to break camp and walk west across the ice, the men carrying two 20 foot lifeboats along as they went. Shackleton's biographer said that the cold and hunger were daunting, but nothing could compare to the relentless darkness of the winter of 1915.

Tim Keller has written, "There is no desolation more complete than the polar night. Only those who have experienced it can fully appreciate what it means to be without the sun day after day and week after week. Few unaccustomed to it can fight off its affects altogether, and it has driven some men mad. In such deep darkness you can't see forward, so you don't know where you're going. You have no direction. You can't even see yourself, you don't know what you look like. You may as well have no identity. And you can't tell whether there is anyone around you, friend or foe. You are isolated …..and disoriented."[64]

Think how this description of physical darkness compares to spiritual darkness. Spiritual darkness paralyzes and leaves us directionless. It leads to constant wandering—with no way to measure progress. Spiritual darkness robs us of our personal identity and sense of worth. It isolates us, whispering that there is no one to help. It crushes us with regret, guilt, and anxiety for the future. This is the trap that Satan relentlessly holds us in. For some the pain is almost unbearable. With unending force Satan assails his prey, driving us toward hopelessness. If the forces of darkness can succeed in driving hope from a person, it's over.

What It Means to be Lost

When we invite darkness into our life, we will find ourselves caught in Satan's trap. We are just deceiving ourselves if we think we can somehow outsmart him. When he snatches us, a myriad of emotions fills our mind. This usually starts with a period of denial. But later, the harsh reality *always* sets in. What will we do in this moment? How will we handle our new reality? Maybe no one else knows our situation. Do we continue to conceal it, hoping that we can somehow fix it on our own? Or, do we seek help? Do we give into Satan who relentlessly says *just fix it on your own and keep it to yourself. Don't let it out, you can't trust anyone to help, they'll just criticize. And if you tell them, you can't bear the awful consequences that await.*

I wonder if this was part of the process with the prodigal son in Luke 15. The treachery of his demand for an early inheritance might be missed with modern readers, but inside Jewish culture his actions would have been clearly understood. In essence, this man was saying he no longer wished to be governed by his father's rule and he would be better off if his father were dead! He was headstrong and rebellious. He couldn't be bothered with doing things right. The principles of respect and honor were outdated. He *deserved* to do what he wanted and *when* he wanted to do it. Self was governing the throne of his heart. When he *finally* got *his* money, he set off for a foreign land and wasted his inheritance on *prodigal* living, 15.13. Times must have been fast and fun. They always are when you are living on the devil's dime. Then it happened. It always does. A famine came and all his fair weather friends were gone, along with all the money. "He began to be in need." 15.14. I think it is here where he is beginning to understand the gravity of his problem, but still thinks he can fix the problem himself. "So he went and hired himself out to one of the citizens of that country, who sent him into his fields to feed pigs. And he was longing to be fed with the pods that the pigs ate, and no one gave him anything." Luke 15.15-16. At this point, the young prodigal is very sorrowful for what's happened. He is probably filled with regret, but make no mistake—self is very much still on the throne of his heart. There is no way he was going to tell anyone else he was wrong.

Is it any different for us? What about the moment when we realize we are caught in Satan's trap? Fear begins to set in. *What am I going to do? How can I fix this? What if someone finds out?* We desperately want to be extricated, but the problem remains. We feel completely alone. Darkness says, *no one* can help. *No one* would understand and if they found out they would never look at us the same. So we get busy relying on our own power and resources to solve things. There's only one problem. Every avenue we pursue and every solution we think will work leads only to more problems. Our stress and pain increase to unimaginable levels. We work and work, coming up with one scheme and plan after another, but nothing turns out. The frustration grows and its toll becomes intense. Before long, those we love most are forced to suffer along with us as they deal with the brunt of anger, piercing words, and damaged relationships. This is not a *fun* place to be.

All the while as we flail around, desperately trying to "fix" the situation, there is, in the back of our mind, an impending sense of doom. The vicious cycle we have created has now morphed into a downward spiral. All the while, we are forced to keep a smile on our face and tell ourselves that somehow, someway we will be exempt from the inevitable. *We're different. The rules do not apply to us.* We are *really not* the hypocrite that we feel like. Self is still on the throne of our heart. Whether or not we realize it, during these moments, darkness is still thriving inside of us. We may feel that we've moved closer, but the original problem remains....*we're caught inside Satan's trap.* We just *can't* get out, **no matter how hard we try.**

Then, it happens. The bottom falls out. The weight of our problems crushes every hollow wall we've built. Suddenly, **everything** comes crashing down. Maybe it is one event, or multiple ones. When the first blow comes, we wonder how we could ever handle anything else, but then another one comes that takes us even lower. One by one the blows continue to come. We are powerless. Our strength is depleted. Hope is quickly fading. All the while darkness cheers in the background and Satan smiles and laughs. He has now taken the knife he used to kill us with and is gleefully twisting it.

Now, at the lowest point, there is no way to go but up. We are completely broken and crushed. We are desperate. There is no power left. There are no personal resources that can fix the problem. It has entered into the realm of the *impossible*. Thinking about the prodigal son again, I wonder if something happened we are not told about finally that caused him to *come to his senses*. Was it just the sheer hunger and cold loneliness that drove him out of his desperate state? Between Luke 15.16 and 17, *something* must have driven him to the understanding that his problem was bigger than he could ever fix. With every last ounce of mental and emotional strength he could muster he reasoned within himself, "How many of my father's hired servants have more than enough bread, but I perish here with hunger." 15.17. Hear the desperation in his voice. See the look on his face. Feel his grief. *I have got to get help. I can't do this anymore.*

So, he turns to the only place he knew he could go. "I will arise and go to my father, and I will say to him, 'Father, I have sinned against heaven and before you. I am no longer worthy to be called your son. Treat me as one of your hired servants.'" 15.18-19. **Finally**, he had the courage to kick Satan out of his life. **Finally**, he had the courage to go home. **Finally**, he had replaced "self" with God as the primary influence in his life. *Now*, he was inviting God back into this heart.

We Need to Get Back to the Gospel

What we have just read is the condition of being lost. How many understand the awfulness of what it means to be lost? Do we know individuals who are caught on a ride they desperately want to get off and find the closest exit? How many have reached a point where their hope is fading? Think of all of those who are still living in denial, being led on by Satan? They're all around us. Look up and see the darkness all around. We must reflect the light of Christ into their life.

How many Christians have forgotten their former condition? *We* were were lost. *We* made bad decisions. *We* bore awful consequences. *We* blamed others. *We* broke God's heart, **over and over again.** We were in a *desperate* situation! Paul described us as "enemies of God." Romans 5.6-10. It's only by God's immeasurable grace and mercy that we are still breathing. We stand by the grace of God and continual power of Jesus. Keeping this in mind will help us to develop a full appreciation for the love of God and His incredible desire to rescue us from Satan's grasp. And, it should generate within us an undying passion to share the precious message of salvation with everyone we can.

The gospel *(good news)* begins with a *personal* response in recognition of our hopeless situation, which can only be remedied by the action of God. Its climax is reached in Jesus' death on the cross and resurrection from the dead, 1 Corinthians 15.3-4. Sin is so hideous that it required the death of the Son of God. Only God could reach us. There was no other way. We must act on our belief through repentance and confession and die to our former self through the waters of baptism, Romans 6.1-16.

Preaching this simple message can be very effective today, just as it was during the first century. The apostles clearly taught what it means to be lost and then shared the remedy by preaching Jesus. Acts 2, 3, 8 and 17 are four examples. When their audiences heard the apostles' preaching and understood their lost condition, those who accepted it, obeyed. Saving faith is an active faith that responds to the work of God in providing us salvation. Let's allow Jesus to do His work through us and draw all men unto Him, John 12.32. Just like the apostles, today we show the lost their need for *Jesus!* Because of what Jesus accomplished on the cross, He will deliver every person who responds to His great invitation. **No one is out of His reach!**

Conclusion

Shackleton's expedition finally landed on Elephant Island after 497 days being at sea. Their harrowing experience stands as one of the most incredible adventure stories of all time. Can you imagine having lived through such an experience? Once you were delivered and wound up back home, how would you have viewed the simple pleasure of a warm summer's day, basking in the glowing sunlight? Would you not have appreciated that in a way you never would have before?

New Testament Christians have been delivered from the grasp of Satan. We were once in the pit, trapped in the mire, and doomed for eternal destruction. But, in His tender mercy and pity, God looked down on us and *rescued* us. Now, what will we do with our new status? Will we seek to point the way out for anyone who is lost? Will we appreciate what it means to be a son or daughter of God? Will we live each day with a sense of thankfulness and appreciation? Will we resolve to no longer walk in our former ways, allowing the Holy Spirit to fill our life with the ways of God? The choice is yours. Will you let God's light into your life?

For Thought and Reflection:

- What emotions have filled your mind when you have first realized you are caught in Satan's trap?

- Why is it so tempting to listen to Satan and follow his suggestion to *just fix things on our own?*

- Describe the feelings of loneliness that are associated with being caught in Satan's trap.

- As we try to "fix the problem," how can others around us be affected?

- Why is it so easy to believe that somehow *the rules don't apply* to us. That *we're different from everyone else?*

- Have you ever had *everything come crashing down?* Describe how it felt as you were crushed by your sin.

- Why does it seem that sometimes it takes us sinking to the lowest of depths before we *come to our senses?*

- What is the message of the gospel?

- Do you think we have changed the focus of the gospel message and diluted its power? Why or Why not?

- Read the sermons in Acts 2, 3, 8, and 17. What was the starting point of the message of the Apostles and evangelists of the first century?

- What happens when we preach the gospel in its undiluted form? See Romans 1.16-17.

Endnotes

1   The Week (October 20, 2010). "Chilean miners: What happened in the first 17 days?" Retrieved 11/18/2011 from: http://theweek.com/article/index/208372/chilean-miners-what-happened-in-the-first-17-days.

2   Quinones, J., Orso, A., Katrandjian, O., (October 18, 2010). "Exclusive: Chilean Miner Dubbed 'Super Mario' Speaks Out". Retrieved 11/18/2011 from: http://abcnews.go.com/GMA/chilean-miner-mario-sepulveda-dubbed-super-mario-speaks/story?id=11904199#.TsbCO2D-Gdoo

3   Orr, J. (1915). Darkness. International Standard Bible Encyclopedia. (Accordance). Alamonte Springs, FL: Oak Tree Software.

4   MacArthur, J. (1986). Ephesians: MacArthur New Testament Commentary. Chicago: Moody Publishers.

5   Vergara, E., (August 3, 2011). "Reality tarnishes myth of Chile's 33 rescued miners." Retrieved 11/18/2011 from http://www.msnbc.msn.com/id/44009279/ns/world_news-americas/t/reality-tarnishes-myth-chiles-rescued-miners/#.TscbPWDGeJU

6   McCullum, H. (2010). Somalia: Faint hope for a failed state. Retrieved 12/1/2011 from http://www.africafiles.org/article.asp?id=7586

7   Fausset, A.R. (1878). Calf Worship. Fausset's Bible Dictionary.

8   Isaiah 60.19-22

9   Jeremiah 31.33; Ezekiel 11.33

10   Genesis 3.14-15

11   Renner, R. (2009). Darkness Cannot Overcome the Light. Retreived 12/1/2011 from http://www.crosswalk.com/faith/spiritual-life/darkness-cannot-overcome-the-light-11604075.html

12   ibid

13   MacArthur, J. (1986). Ephesians: MacArthur New Testament Commentary. Chicago: Moody Publishers.

14   Skate (2011). "Christopher Hitchens Remembered." Retrieved 12/17/2011 from http://www.slate.com/articles/news_and_politics/fighting_words/2011/12/tributes_to_the_journalist_and_intellectual_from_julian_barnes_anne_applebaum_james_fenton_and_others_.html

15   McClelland, S. (2011, December 17). "Tebow backlash now in full force." Dayton Daily News. pp. C2

16 O'Connor, C. (2000). Personal Interview. Retrieved 12/17/2011 from http://www.youtube.com/watch?v=daZ0aKB9jng

17 Sitcom reviews from Plugged In Online. Retrieved 12/17/2011 from http://www.pluggedin.com/tv.aspx

18 MacArthur, J. (1989). Freedom from Sin. Retrieved 12/17/2011 from: http://www.gty.org/resources/Positions/P13/Freedom-from-Sin

19 Gibbons, J. (2011). "The Awfulness of Sin." The Sword and Staff. 49:4. p. 4.

20 MacArthur J. (1977, January 9). "Sin" Grace to You. Retrieved 11/15/2011 from http://www.gty.org/resources/sermons/1247/sin

21 As seen in the KJV and NKJV. The NASU says, "There are things under the ban in your midst."

22 MacArthur J. (1977, January 9). "Sin" Grace to You. Retrieved 11/15/2011 from http://www.gty.org/resources/sermons/1247/sin

23 Nixon, R. (1974 August 9)."Final Remarks to the White House Staff." Retrieved 1/4/2012 from http://watergate.info/nixon/74-08-09final-remarks.shtml

24 Hill, J. H. (1934). From Joshua to David. Nashville: Convention Press. 97.

25 Chadwell, D. (2005). ""The Contrast." David: the Man After God's Own Heart. Retrieved 01/04/2012 from http://www.westarkchurch.org/chadwell/david/teaching/y2005q4l1.htm.

26 ibid.

27 Norman, J. (2010). "Tucker Carlson: Michael Vick Deserves to Die." Retrieved 01/12/2012 from http://www.cbsnews.com/8301-31751_162-20026769-10391697.html

28 Brown, J. (2009) "Michael Vick's '60 Minutes' Interview" Atlanta Journal-Constitution. Retrieved 01/12/2012 from http://www.ajc.com/sports/michael-vicks-60-minutes-116871.html

29 Video of Vick's '60 Minutes' Interview can be found here: http://www.cbsnews.com/video/watch/?id=5245553n&tag=mncol;list;1

30 Florio, M. (2010). "Vick Calls Prison 'The Best Thing That Ever Happened to Me.'" ProFootball Talk. Retrieved 01/12/2012 from http://profootballtalk.nbcsports.com/2010/10/03/vick-calls-prison-the-best-thing-that-ever-happened-to-me/

31 Wilson, P. (2012). "Breaking the Silence." Without Wax. Retrieved 01/09/2012 from http://withoutwax.tv/2012/01/09/breaking-the-silence/

32 Lucado, M. (2002). "When You Can't Hide Your Mistakes." Up Words. http://www.maxlucado.com

[33] Graham, B. (1997) "Confession of Sins" The Bible Doctrine of Sin. Temple Terrace: Florida College Press. 126.

[34] Lucado.

[35] Heck, V (2012). "Vick's Probation Almost Over." Yahoo Sports. Retrieved 01/12/2012 from http://sports.yahoo.com/nfl/news?slug=ycn-10825531

[36] National Park Service (2011). "The Jasper Fire." Jewell Cave National Monument. Retrieved 01/26/2012 from http://www.nps.gov/jeca/naturescience/jasperfire.htm

[37] USA TODAY (2004). "Why Do We Speed? Because Everyone Else Does, Especially Our Leaders." Retrieved 01/25/2012 from http://www.usatoday.com/news/nation/2004-04-10-speed1_x.htm

[38] Hetland, C. (2004). "The Accident and the Aftermath." Minnesota Public Radio. Retrieved 01/25/2012 from http://news.minnesota.publicradio.org/features/2004/01/21_hetlandc_janklowfive/

[39] Piper, J. (2001). "There is Law!" Desiring God. Retrieved 01/17/2012 from http://www.desiringgod.org/resource-library/sermons/the-importance-of-knowing-our-sin

[40] Barnes' Notes on the New Testament. Public Domain. Derived from an electronic text from the Christian Classics Ethereal Library <http://www.ccel.org>. Formatted and corrected by OakTree Software, Inc. Version 1.3.

[41] Piper, J. (2001). "How Do We Come to Know Sin?" Desiring God. Retrieved 01/17/2012 from http://www.desiringgod.org/resource-library/sermons/how-we-come-to-know-sin

[42] Piper.

[43] Kaus, A (2011). "Janklow has been given four tickets since fatal crash in 2003." The Daily Republic. Retrieved 01/25/2011 from http://www.mitchellrepublic.com/event/article/id/55592/

[44] Eisenhower Memorial (2012). "Ike and the Death Camps." Retrieved 02/02/2012 from http://www.eisenhowermemorial.org/stories/death-camps.htm

[45] BBC (2005 December 14). "Iranian leader denies Holocaust." BBC. Retrieved 02/02/2012 from http://news.bbc.co.uk/2/hi/middle_east/4527142.stm

[46] Ridgeway, J. (2007). "Homeland Insecurity: The 9/11 Conspiracy File: Myths and Facts." Mother Jones. Retrieved 02/02/2012 from: http://motherjones.com/politics/2007/09/homeland-insecurity-911-conspiracy-file-myths-and-facts

[47] Hendrickson, W. (2002). New Testament Commentary: John. Grand Rapids, MI: Baker. p. 246.

[48] Hendrickson. p. 379.

[49] See Mishna in "Sanhedrin" Volume 1.

[50] See Mishna in "Sanhedrin" Volume 4.

[51] Hendrickson. p.396.

[52] Associated Press (2012 February 7). "Missing Utah woman Susan Powell was murdered, authorities acknowledge for first time. Oregon Live. Retreived 02/12/2012 from http://www.oregonlive.com/pacific-northwest-news/index.ssf/2012/02/missing_utah_woman_susan_powel.html

[53] ibid.

[54] This note from the Life Application Bible lists out the 10 instances where Israel rebelled against God during their travels through the wilderness: God wasn't exaggerating when he said that the Israelites had "again and again" failed to trust and obey him. Here is a list of their failures: (1) lacking trust at the crossing of the Red Sea (Exodus 14:11, 12); (2) complaining over bitter water at Marah (Exodus 15:24); (3) complaining in the wilderness of Sin (Exodus 16:3); (4) collecting more than the daily quota of manna (Exodus 16:20); (5) collecting manna on the Sabbath (Exodus 16:27-29); (6) complaining over lack of water at Rephidim (Exodus 17:2, 3); (7) engaging in idolatry with a golden calf (Exodus 32:7-10); (8) complaining at Taberah (Numbers 11:1, 2); (9) more complaining over the lack of delicious food (Numbers 11:4); (10) failing to trust God and enter the Promised Land (Numbers 14:1-4).
Life Application Study Bible (Accordance electronic ed. Carol Stream: Tyndale House Publishers, 2004), n.p.

[55] Vine, W. E. "Hard, Harden, Hardening, Hardness", Vine's Expository Dictionary of New Testament Words. Blue Letter Bible. 1940. 24 June, 1996 10 Feb 2012.
<http://www.blueletterbible.org/Search/Dictionary/viewTopic.cfm? type=GetTopic&Topic=Hard,+Harden,+Hardening,+Hardness& DictList=9#Vine's>

[56] Morgan, R. "Nelson's Complete Book of Stories."

[57] Webster, A (2005). "If I Don't Preach on Hell, Pt. 1). Glad Tidings of Good Things. Jacksonville Church of Christ, Jacksonville, AL: p. 2.

[58] Keller, T. (2003) "The Importance of Hell." Redeemer.com. Retrieved 02/16/2012 from http://www.redeemer.com/news_and_events/articles/ the_importance_of_hell.html

[59] Barna, G. (2011). "Top Trends of 2011: Changing Role of Christianity. The Barna Group. Retrieved 02/16/2012 from http://www.barna.org/faith-spirituality/543-top-trends-of-2011-changing-role-of-christianity?q=hell

[60] Webster.

[61] On February 18, 2012, the state of New Jersey ordered all flags in the state to be set at half mast in honor of singer Whitney Houston, who died on February 12, 2012.

[62] Piper, J. (1998). "The Final Divide: Eternal Life or Eternal Death, Part 1." Desiring God. Retrieved 02/17/2012 from http://www.desiringgod.org/resource-library/sermons/the-final-divide-eternal-life-or-eternal-wrath-part-1

[63] View the trailer for "Hell and Mr. Fudge" at http://www.hellandmrfudge.com/

[64] Keller, T (2011). King's Cross: The story of the world in the life of Jesus. Penguin Press. Retrieved 11/15/2011 from http://books.google.com/books?id=hhUDWECTYA8C&pg=PT147&dq=Coming+Out+of+Spiritual+Darkness&hl=en&ei=yOTGTope0uWCB_y7wVU&sa=X&oi=book_result&ct=result&resnum=7&ved=0CE0Q6AEwBg#v=onepage&q=Coming%20Out%20of%20Spiritual%20Darkness&f=false

For a full listing of our books, visit DeWard's website:

www.deward.com